Merrily's Border

Merrily's Border

THE MYSTERIOUS WORLD OF
Merrily Watkins
HISTORY & FOLKLORE
PEOPLE & PLACES

Phil Rickman
PHOTOS BY **John Mason**

LOGASTON PRESS

FRONT COVER: The Queen Stone © John Mason
(NB The Queen Stone stands on private land and is not publicly accessible)
BACK COVER, LEFT TO RIGHT: West End Farmhouse, Pembridge © Andy Johnson; Edward Elgar; King Arthur's Cave © John Mason
FRONTISPIECE: Yew tree in the churchyard at Hay Church © John Mason

Logaston Press, The Holme, Church Road, Eardisley, Herefordshire HR3 6NJ
An imprint of Fircone Books Ltd.
www.logastonpress.co.uk

First edition 2009. Second edition 2013.
This edition first published 2018. Reprinted with minor amendments 2022.

ISBN 978-1-910839-30-0

Text copyright © Phil Rickman, 2018.
All images copyright © John Mason unless otherwise credited in Acknowledgements on p. VI.

All rights reserved.
The moral right of the author has been asserted.

Without limiting the rights under copyright reserved above, no part of this publication may be reproduced, stored in or introduced into a retrieval system, or transmitted, in any form or by any means (electronic, mechanical, photocopying, recording or otherwise), without prior written permission of the copyright owner and the above publisher of this book.

Designed and typeset by Richard Wheeler.
Cover design by Richard Wheeler.

Printed and bound in Poland.

Logaston Press is committed to a sustainable future for our business, our readers and our planet.
The book in your hands is made from paper from sustainable sources.

British Library Catalogue in Publishing Data.
A CIP catalogue record for this book is available from the British Library.

CONTENTS

	Acknowledgements	vi
	Preface	vii
	Map	viii
	Introduction	1
1	Old Cider	5
2	Something a Bit Dark	15
3	Midwinter	21
4	Witchlights	31
5	Lady of the Bines	39
6	A Dark Lamp	45
7	A Real Creeper	53
8	A Place to Die For	61
9	Music of the Spheres	69
10	Ghosts and Templars	77
11	The Uncoiling of the Serpent	87
12	Gods of War	95
13	The Keys to the Kingdom	107
14	A Deviant Burial	127
15	Dance the Darkness Down	135
16	Wanderer through the Woods	143
17	The Others	155
	The Merrily Watkins Series	161
	Select Bibliography	162
	Index	164

View to Radnor Forest from Old Radnor

ACKNOWLEDGEMENTS

Thanks are given to the following for the photographs and illustrations used in this book. To John Mason for the majority of the photographs used, including the front cover image. All photographs are copyright John Mason unless otherwise stated below. Thanks to Andy Johnson for the photographs on pages 6, 7, 12 (top left), 25, 26, 28, 31, 32 (top), 33, 34, 37 (top), 40, 41, 46, 47, 49, 51, 52, 56, 69, 70, 71, 72, 74, 88, 92, 96 (top two), 112 (bottom right), 157 and 158; to Richard Wheeler for the photographs on pages 4 and 153; to Ken Hutchinson for the maps on pages VIII and 24; to Andy Stevenson for the photograph on page 11; to Cally for the photograph of Nick Drake on page 13; to Phil Rickman for the photograph on page 19; to Lawrence Hurley for the photograph of the carving in All Saints Church on page 29; to Tony Williams courtesy of Maureen Beauchamp and the Derek Foxton Collection for the hop-pickers on pages 43 and 44; to Katherina Garratt-Adams for the photograph on page 58; to Watkins and Thomas Estate Agents for the photograph on page 73 (bottom right); to John Bullough for the photograph on page 89; and to Bev Craven for the reworking of the image of John Dee on page 159. The image of the painting of E.M. Leather on page 9 is courtesy of John Simons.

    A lot of people are due thanks for help putting together the Merrily Watkins stories, and most are credited in various novels. Ced Jackson and Richard Bartholomew, of the British Society of Dowsers, provided extra information for this book, along with various deliverance consultants and ministers, some named, some preferring not to be. Thanks, finally, to Richard & Su Wheeler of Logaston Press for their work on this edition.

Bredwardine Bridge across the Wye

PREFACE

THIS BOOK is a result of all the letters and emails which come in daily from readers who say how *real* the Merrily Watkins series feels.

I can't claim too much of the credit for that. As John Mason's pictures demonstrate, virtually all the locations are real, even if some smaller communities are protected by fictional names. And so is much of the background: actual history, legend, folklore and customs, overlaid by recent and current issues.

Essentially, this is a guide to some of the more mysterious elements along the mid and southern Welsh Border. Researching the novels takes me into some areas which seem never to have been fully explored before – certainly not in fiction. You might also find material here which has never appeared in a guide book either. What happens ... putting together a novel, you find yourself drawing together disparate threads, and then, suddenly, you're looking at a whole new tapestry.

As you can imagine, it's quite difficult to make a book like this work without giving away key elements of the fictional plots, but I've tried not to reveal details which might spoil anything for new readers of the novels. To avoid any of those *look away now* moments, information is, just occasionally, incomplete ... although, where possible, other sources are indicated for readers who want to know more.

But, even if you haven't read any of the novels and don't intend to, this book will give you different perspectives on Herefordshire and neighbouring parts of Shropshire, Radnorshire and the Forest of Dean ... areas either side of the Welsh Border which, even when you think you know them, will gradually disclose whole layers of mystery. The Select Bibliography opens up further avenues of exploration.

Phil Rickman

Introduction

A Border Thing

Borders. For as long as I can remember I've been drawn to them, this one in particular. Borders are risky places, where the unexpected happens. As a kid in Lancashire, an hour or so's drive from Wales, I used to fantasize about what it would be like living on the border. *Right* on the border. One foot in England, one foot in Wales – how would that *feel*?

That was before I'd learned of the very real mystique around borders, the suggestion that a geographical frontier might also be the division between different states of mind, different ways of thinking ... even (careful, now ...) different levels of existence.

Anyway, for most of my adult life, I've lived very close either to the Welsh border or the English border, depending on your standpoint, passing almost daily between the two nations, in an area which is superficially serene but still smouldering with history and clouded with folklore. And now I'm writing novels exploring its textures; a series of novels which seem to have created their own fictional genre; mysteries with more than one layer of mystery.

Mysteries – or so I like to think – in the original sense. The Merrily novels are a combination of the crime thriller and the possibilities of *something else*. Even today, surprisingly few people, locals or incomers, scorn belief in the paranormal. They'll smile sometimes, but they won't scoff.

The series is centred on Herefordshire, extending into Radnor Forest, the hills of Shropshire and Monmouthshire, the Black Mountains and the Malverns. The history and legends of each location tend to invade the stories, along with current issues, and in the end I'm always surprised at how little needs to be made up.

Opposite: Map of the area

This is a fringe area, in many ways neither England nor Wales, always thinly populated and thus largely ignored by national and regional media. It's always had secrets and usually been able to keep them. The Welsh leader, Owain Glyndwr was last heard of not in the mountains of north Wales but in the Golden Valley of Herefordshire. Salman Rushdie, under Islamic death-sentence, was successfully hidden near Brecon. It's even been rumoured that Lord Lucan, on the run after the murder of his children's nanny, found temporary shelter on the edge of Offa's Dyke before leaving the country.

Less furtively, there was Arthur Conan Doyle tracking the Hound of the Baskervilles, Edward Elgar on his bike, Alfred Watkins sighting ancient tracks between standing stones and steeples.

Today, rock stars and royals find sanctuary here. That famous face you think you saw in Leominster or somewhere ... well, it probably was. This is a safe haven for the famous and the notorious – nobody gets too excited. As my friend Gomer Parry once said, 'En't a problem for us, boy. Long as they don't get too cosy with the sheep.'

Gomer Parry. In many ways, this man *is* the Border. Old but ageless, built like a thorn tree on a hillside facing the west wind, Gomer has hair like a battered lavatory brush, wears thick glasses, smokes roll-ups. Raised in upland, subsistence farming, Gomer decided – long before it became a Government buzz-word – that it was time to diversify.

So he went into Plant Hire. Bought himself a second-hand JCB with which to dig field drains and soakaways for septic tanks. It gave him a certain status, the freedom of the countryside and the ability to crush lesser vehicles with one swing of the bucket. Also a good living because, as he often points out, 'fields is always gonner need draining and if your soakaway don't soak away you're in deep ... trouble.'

Gomer was born in old Radnorshire, at the time the least-known and least-populated county in southern Britain. When my wife, Carol and I were working there as journalists we encountered him – memorably – several times. He's an independent man who observes the natural laws of the countryside and the rules of Plant Hire – digger chivalry. Most of the time he hates the council, the Government and particularly the shiny-arsed townies who run DEFRA (young Jane Watkins says it stands for Destroying Every Farm-Reared Animal – Gomer likes that).

It took me a while to get to know Gomer, and it was a few years before I felt qualified to write about him, having observed his basic rule for survival on the Border: keep real quiet till you knows the score.

Surprising how many people get that one wrong and wind up face-down in the old slurry pit.

The first Merrily Watkins novel, *The Wine of Angels*, was to have been a Gomer Parry novel until a pivotal aspect of the plot made it necessary for the village of Ledwardine to have a woman vicar.

After which, Merrily, in her insecure, self-effacing, less-than-confident way, took over.

In the next novel, *Midwinter of the Spirit*, she was appointed diocesan exorcist for Hereford and became a series. Now, if you Google exorcism/ Hereford in the hope of finding someone to help you over some domestic intrusion you can't rationally explain, I'm afraid you're likely to be directed, at some stage, to Merrily Watkins.

She's embarrassed, of course. Merrily isn't into fame or the cult-of-personality. This wasn't at all what she had in mind when she arrived in the village of Ledwardine as a thirty-something widow with a slightly resentful teenage daughter, Jane, who at first didn't want to be here and definitely didn't want her mum to be a vicar, not least because her own spiritual leanings were distinctly pagan.

To be honest, I never imagined anyone could write a whole series of fairly dark crime novels from the point of view of a country vicar, female or male. I had no idea, back then, that she was going to turn, quite rapidly, into the best idea I'd ever had.

1   Old Cider

Twisty old devil.
Looked as if it held a grudge in every scabby branch, and
it wouldn't give you any fruit, on principle. Because, left to
rot, apple trees ...
                                      ... they grows resentful.
Merrily's grandad had told her that once, when she was a little
girl. Frightening her ...
                                                                The Wine of Angels

Like most vicars, Merrily is from Off. She has ancestry in the area, but did her training in Liverpool. She's a thirty-something widow with a teenage daughter. She smokes. When she drops something on her foot she doesn't say, 'Oh, bother'. And, no, she *doesn't* look like Dawn French.

Bringing in a stranger is always a useful device for a novelist. After all, most of the readers are also going to be from Off, so viewing an area through the eyes of an outsider lets you dwell on its eccentricities, highlighting both appealing blemishes and sinister stains which locals might no longer notice.

The village of Ledwardine is the missing location on the Herefordshire Black and White Trail. Think timber-framing and white plaster. Think Pembridge, Weobley, Dilwyn, Eardisland; Ledwardine has bits of all of them. It used to be a working village, sustained by farming and the cider industry, but its current prosperity is largely a result of its olde worlde appeal. Here's what it says on a notorious website – www.getalife/welshborder.co.uk (*The Relocation Bible*) – sponsored by estate agents keen to persuade wealthy folk from Off to move in:

LEDWARDINE

Once known as The Village in the Orchard, this community may have begun as simply that. The old centre of the village is still partly enclosed by the remains of an apple orchard dating back at least to medieval times, as do some of its black and white timber-framed houses. Earlier settlement is suggested by recent archaeological discoveries at the foot of Cole Hill, whose Iron Age fortifications are a reminder of a turbulent past. Today, Ledwardine ('Jewel of The New Cotswolds' – *Daily Telegraph*) is serene and inviting. The cobbled village square, with its small, open market-hall supported by oak pillars, is enlivened by a variety of retail outlets, including a bookshop, gallery and delicatessen, as well as the 15th-century Black Swan Inn, noted for its fine food.
FACILITIES: the village, although largely self-sufficient, is a mere ten minute drive from the nearest town of Leominster and no more than twenty-five minutes from the progressive cathedral city of Hereford, now undergoing extensive commercial renewal. Several highly reputable private schools are within easy reach.
LEDWARDINE STAR-RATING **** *and rising!*
WE SAY: *buy now*, while prices are competitive and this area is still relatively obscure.

West Street, Pembridge

Clockwise from above: New Inn, Pembridge; the belfry, Pembridge; Weobley Church; West End Farmhouse, Pembridge; Unicorn House, Weobley

Note the Orchard, central to *The Wine of Angels* and, nine books later, *To Dream of the Dead*. Like many apparently-innocuous features of the border, it's more than it seems. When Merrily arrives in Ledwardine, as priest-in-charge, there's blood on the apple trees and more trouble to come. Incomers to Ledwardine are promoting a summer festival designed to raise the village's prominence on the tourist map and revive the traditional local cider. Meanwhile, the truth is about to be uncovered about a seventeenth-century vicar accused of witchcraft. Then a teenage girl goes missing – and not the first.

This book is full of apples. Apples and cider, apples and murder, apples and the unseen. For example, as the old folklorist Lucy Devenish explains to Jane Watkins, if you cut an apple crossways – that is, not through the stalk – you'll find ...

'There.' She held out a half in the palm of each hand. 'What do you see?'

Jane leaned over the counter. The green-white pulp was veined with thin green lines and dots which made a kind of wheel.

'Count the spokes,' Lucy said.

'Five.'

'It makes a five-pointed star, you see? Inside a circle. A pentagram ... a very ancient symbol of purification and protection. And there's one at the heart of every apple. That says something, doesn't it?'

Lucy Devenish runs a small, crowded shop called Ledwardine Lore, which provides exactly what it says on the sign. Lucy knows more than anybody about the village's secrets, many of which relate to —

Cider

Which, in Herefordshire, goes back, almost certainly, to pre-Roman times, although the Romans apparently preferred perry (the equivalent, made from pears). It's been in and out of fashion ever since, always popular with farm-workers, occasionally favoured by the gentry, especially in the eighteenth century. There are still said to be nearly ten thousand acres of cider orchard in the county. Several independent cider companies are still based there, while Hereford's best-known cider firm, Bulmers, has changed hands twice recently, with owners from Off replaced by owners from seriously Off. You can find out how the wine of angels was originally made in the cider museum by the side of Sainsbury's. A shadowy place with the dense musky atmosphere I wanted the novel to carry.

I've always enjoyed discovering a weird underside to familiar items – the poisoned apple, the worm in the apple – so it was good to find someone of a similar mind, even if long dead. Much of the folklore in this novel and several of the others was plucked from the pages of an invaluable book by —

Ella Mary Leather

Published in 1912, Mrs Leather's *The Folk-lore of Herefordshire* may be the best collection of local legends and traditions ever published in Britain. At least, I've never found one more detailed. This inquisitive Victorian lady (born in 1874) hung out with gypsies and old farm-workers and burrowed deep into the red border soil to uncover half-buried pagan roots, customs, traditions, superstitions, folk tales, folk song ... the rhythm and pulse of the Border.

'No record in cold print can give the reader an idea of the pleasure experienced in collecting the elusive material we call folk lore from the living brains of men and women of whose lives it has formed an integral part,' she writes in her preface, after relating how it all began with Martha B —

> ... a tiny, dark-haired, olive skinned woman who, when I first remembered her, gathered apples in a Herefordshire orchard ... Martha smoked a little clay pipe, apologetically 'by doctor's orders'; her greeting was always 'Good day, missie, God bless you'; I learned that this formula was an infallible protection against witchcraft and the evil eye. It was Martha who could tell how the house which once stood in the wood had been pulled down because it was so badly haunted; she herself saw ghosts and could point out the very spots where they appeared to her.

Mrs Leather was from Weobley, a place very close to Ledwardine. If she'd been born 50 years later, she would almost certainly have been Lucy Devenish's best friend.

The only book to pick up Mrs Leather's trail in recent years is Roy Palmer's *Herefordshire Folklore*, part of his valuable and timely series, which also deals with Radnorshire, Shropshire, Monmouthshire and Worcestershire. Arguably, still the most mysterious area of southern Britain.

On the advice of Ella Mary, I called the original Ledwardine cider apple the Pharisees Red – the 'pharisees' a corruption of *farises*, an archaic local word for fairies, whose tiny lights, according to legend, may be seen in the Ledwardine orchard, along with bits of old Edgar Powell, who blows his head off with a 12-bore shotgun during an attempted revival of —

Wassailing

This is a custom usually carried out on Twelfth Night in an attempt to ensure a good crop of apples the following autumn. It's been revived in Herefordshire over the past 20 years, with wassails in Much Marcle in the east and Eardisley in the west. In can involve pouring cider over the roots of an apple tree or, as in *The Wine of Angels*, firing shotguns through the branches after an appropriately encouraging chant.

The Twelfth Night ceremonies may have begun with the lighting of fires in wheat fields to encourage healthy crops. The lighting up of the darkest time of the year. The pagan origins are clear. Mrs Leather also describes a ritual I just had to borrow, which seems to get inside the earth itself.

> The men stand in a ring around the fire and 'holloa auld cider'. They sing on one very deep note, very slowly, holding each syllable as long as possible, 'Auld–Ci–der.' The 'der' becomes a sort of growl at the end and is an octave below the first two notes; it has a weird dirge-like effect.

Wassailing

The title of this novel comes from the line 'Tears are the wine of angels, the best ... to quench the devil's fires' attributed to a seventeenth-century Herefordshire poet and mystic whose work is often quoted in the book to echo certain themes.

THOMAS TRAHERNE (1637–74)

The son of a Hereford shoemaker, Traherne became Rector of Credenhill several centuries before the SAS moved in. Lucy Devenish was not the only person to have detected elements of paganism or at least pantheism in his poetry.

Essentially, Traherne was a pre-hippy advocate of happiness ... *felicity*. He knew and loved the countryside in all its jewelled moods. His philosophy was, *God gave it to you – enjoy*. In fact, he suggested, *not* enjoying it was an insult to creation, and his lines,

> *You never enjoy the world aright*
> *Till the sea itself floweth in your veins*
> *Till you are clothed in the heavens*
> *And crowned with the stars*

— were memorably set to music, at the zenith of psychedelia, by Mike Heron of The Incredible String Band, who clearly held similar views.

In *The Wine of Angels*, Lucy Devenish introduces Traherne's poems to Lol Robinson, a songwriter and musician who gets closer, with almost every book, to Merrily Watkins. Lol's career in folk-rock, with the band Hazey Jane, was cut short in difficult circumstances. He finds himself relating increasingly to the artist who influenced his earliest songs and provided the band with its name:

NICK DRAKE (1948–74)

Lol is one of the many contemporary singer-songwriters influenced to the point of minor obsession by someone far more famous now than he ever was in his brief lifetime. In a way, Lol, though more than 20 years younger, is what Nick Drake might have become if he'd survived.

Nick's songs, such as 'Way to Blue', 'Hazey Jane II', 'River Man', 'From the Morning', convey a unique sense of wistful, pastoral Englishness. The problem at the time of their release was that there were just so many ground-breaking albums around that it was easy for something this subtle and restrained to fall through the cracks.

The albums had poor sales. It didn't help that Nick himself was becoming increasingly withdrawn and had problems facing an audience. Someone who went to one of his very rare concerts told me he'd physically half-turn himself away from the crowd.

Eventually, it became clear that Nick was becoming mentally ill. He died at his parents' home in Tanworth-in-Arden, in Warwickshire, from an overdose of anti-depressants which may or may not have been accidental. You can hear the chill of despair in his later songs, in the elemental menace of 'Pink Moon' and the raw bleakness of 'Black Eyed Dog'.

Nick Drake

It wasn't until the mid-1990s that Nick's three albums, *Five Leaves Left*, *Bryter Layter* and *Pink Moon*, took off, artists including Paul Weller and Beth Orton having identified him as a major influence. In 2007, after many bootlegs, his early home-recordings, which included his mother Molly's

Opposite, clockwise from top left: Credenhill Church; stained glass in Hereford Cathedral by artist Tom Denny, inspired by Thomas Traherne

own surprisingly effective songs, were finally released as the album *Family Tree*, with sleeve-notes (and a duet on the sadly prophetic cover of 'All My Trials, Soon Be Over') by his sister, the actor Gabrielle Drake.

Around the time of *Family Tree*, I finally went to Tanworth-in-Arden. As did Lol Robinson, in the ninth novel, *The Fabric of Sin*.

Nick shares with his parents, Molly and Rodney, a modest stone under an oak tree in the raised churchyard at Tanworth. It's a lovely spot which will always, for me, carry a soundtrack of 'From the Morning', the soft, summery final song on the final album. For Lol, inevitably, it was more complicated and, with the help of Gabrielle Drake and Cally, who handles Nick's business affairs, we were

Nick Drake's grave

able to catch the moment on the abridged audio book of *Fabsin*. Lol's own collections, *Songs from Lucy's Cottage* and *A Message from the Morning* (music and lyrics by Allan Watson and Phil Rickman), are available as CDs – details on the website www.philrickman.co.uk.

Meanwhile, back in *The Wine of Angels*, Merrily is faced with a series of inexplicable and possibly paranormal events in and around the seventeenth-century crookedly timber-framed vicarage where she and Jane live. She tries to elicit some advice from her employers on how to deal with them, only to find that the Church of England tends to consider the idea of psychic phenomena slightly embarrassing. Slowly, Merrily finds out who her friends are: Lucy Devenish the folklorist, Lol Robinson the songwriter, and Gomer Parry who, in semi-retirement from Plant Hire, digs the graves and looks after the churchyard.

It isn't until the second book, *Midwinter of the Spirit*, that Merrily becomes aware of the deliverance ministry, the Church's secret service.

2 Something a Bit Dark

After *Wine* I couldn't bring myself to dump Merrily. Or Jane. Particularly Jane. But I definitely didn't want to write a series of what are known in the USA as 'clerical mysteries' in which persons of the cloth implausibly investigate cosy murders. If Merrily was to survive, she had to be authentically employed in some area of the job which might realistically involve her with criminal behaviour and the underside of spirituality.

The answer appeared to lie in deliverance. Or, as it was previously known, exorcism – the name having been changed, in the Anglican church, as a result of a horrifyingly frenzied murder.

In 1974, just a year after shocking scenes of demonic possession in the film *The Exorcist* had led to medical alerts in cinemas all over Britain, a 31-year-old unemployed handyman called Michael Taylor, from Ossett, near Barnsley, went to a local minister, claiming to be possessed by devils. Two priests subsequently embarked on an all-night exorcism, after which they told him they'd cast out an estimated 40 demons. Taylor then went home and savagely killed his wife, tearing out her eyes and her tongue.

Within the Church of England, this had repercussions at the highest level. The Archbishop of Canterbury at the time, Donald Coggan, said, 'We must get this business out of the mumbo-jumbo of magic. I think there are many cases where the more rash exorcists have bypassed the work of psychiatrists.'

New rules and new guidelines for exorcists were introduced – followed, 12 years later, by the official casting-out of the term 'exorcism'. Henceforth, each diocese would have a deliverance adviser, whose own advisers should include a psychiatrist. The new watchword was caution, and it still is.

A former deliverance minister in Herefordshire said, 'I always remember my

predecessor saying to me, "This is a mucky world and you come across mucky things. It's not a very nice job. You get a sense of something a bit dark." He was right. You do find strange circumstances and disturbed people. You can actually feel the hairs going up on the back of your neck even while you're looking for the rational explanations.'

Because of increasing demand and the need, these days, always to cover your back, one deliverance minister per diocese is often seen as insufficient. Now it tends to be a team, whose main function is to offer advice and support to local priests faced with aspects of the unexplained in their parishes.

In a big diocese there could be 12 people involved, including psychiatrists. Which means there are now more trained exorcists working in the UK than at any time in the history of the Church ... and this in a so-called secular age.

'We are, in a way, getting more medieval with every year that passes,' says Canon Michael Wadsworth, for some years a member of a deliverance team based at Ely in the Cambridgeshire Fens. 'There's a sense in which secular men and woman tend to believe a lot more – things their grandparents would have thought rubbish. And the difference now is that people want to do something about it.'

I've learned a lot about the procedures and the pitfalls of exorcism in the ten years since the *Merrily Watkins* series began. From the start, I wanted the stories to be absolutely authentic. No gratuitous horror, no hint of fantasy ... and a central character who is flawed, paranoid and doesn't always get it right.

At first, the clergy I approached for background information were understandably suspicious. Then, after the second novel, a deliverance minister – someone I didn't, at the time, know – emailed to say he thought the low-key approach and the balance between the real and the imagined were 'exactly right'. As other approving emails filtered through from what's regarded as the coalface of Christianity, I learned a lot ... and realised that Merrily, with her nicotine habit, her uncertainty and her occasional lapses into language not found in prayer books, wasn't exactly the maverick I'd initially had in mind. Closer, in fact, to the norm.

Deliverance is the Church's secret service, often regarded with suspicion within the C of E, in much the same way as the police mistrust the spooks of Special Branch. Some image-conscious senior clerics see it as a potentially dangerous throwback to the days of the Witchfinder General.

Which may be why deliverance ministers are usually hand-picked by their bishops. Like Merrily, they are often reluctant to take on a role which involves dealing with both human delusion and – even worse – the possibility that some of it *isn't* delusion.

Opposite: the tiny Church of St Mary the Virgin at Capel-y-ffin

The priests who actually volunteer for deliverance work, in the hope of a hand-to-hand scrap with the powers of evil, are the ones considered least suitable for the job. What the Church is looking for, it seems, is a quality of restraint. And, when you need to separate the real from the imagined, a touch of scepticism is also helpful.

'Someone who says "I need to be exorcized" is usually someone looking for an easy answer,' one exorcist told me, and someone who should be handled with protective gloves. But if even alleged spiritual invasion of a person is rare, property is more vulnerable. It's mainly about ghosts.

The two most commonly reported phenomena encountered by the deliverance ministry are poltergeists and what have become known as 'bereavement apparitions' – sightings, usually by close relatives, of the newly-dead.

It's been estimated that one in four bereaved relatives – husbands and wives, sons and daughters – or even work colleagues will catch occasional glimpses of the departed in familiar spots. A deliverance co-ordinator in Herefordshire says it can sometimes become contagious.

'While many will have some hazy experiences of seeing or hearing the person who has died – which will cease – for a few, these continue and become very vivid, especially if the death was unexpected or complicated. Other people close to the bereaved person may come to share these experiences and reinforce the problem of being unable to let go of the dead person.'

This might be treated by an explanatory chat over a cup of tea, and perhaps prayers or, in extreme cases, a Requiem Eucharist – in effect a second funeral service.

But what are we talking about here? Is it an actual ghost or what psychiatrists would call a psychological projection?

The current co-chairman of British exorcism's governing body, the Christian Deliverance Study Group, is the Bishop of Monmouth, Dominic Walker, perhaps Britain's most experienced exorcist.

Bishop Dominic comes across as urbane, laid-back and well practised in the art of understatement. He says he believes that 90 per cent of all apparitions are mental projections, and it takes some prompting to get him to talk about the time he believes he actually stood next to one.

A ghost, that is. A *real* ghost.

A family had moved into a house to find that the upstairs was already occupied by a middle-aged woman with one leg who would appear and then vanish before their eyes. It emerged that a woman had, in fact, committed suicide there not long after having a leg amputated.

Dominic Walker decided to assemble the family for a Requiem Eucharist – a communion service or Anglican mass for the repose of the dead – in the bedroom where the woman had died, using a dressing table as an altar. Contrary to popular belief, ghosts are not actually exorcised in the *get thee hence* sense; the aim is to direct them towards eternal peace.

'And as we were celebrating the mass, she appeared,' the Bishop recalled. 'It wasn't a frightening experience. It just looked as if we'd been joined by someone else, and that person had only one leg. I thought, Either this is *my* psychological projection or I've been set up. It was only at the end of the service that members of the family said to me, "Do you know that when you were praying for her she appeared?"'

Strange, angelic figures appear in a picture I took at Garway

The woman, he says, finally vanished, never to return.

But it isn't always so easy. Sometimes it takes repeated Requiems and aftercare. A woman minister told me of a case where an apparent poltergeist turned into something out of Hitchcock's *Psycho* – a man attacked in the shower looked down to find blood issuing from a cut in his leg.

'I told the couple I wanted to say prayers in the house and then blessed water and salt and blessed each room. Which was fine till I reached the landing between the bedroom and bathroom.

'The back of my neck was crawling, and I felt cold but there was no draught, and I realised how hard it was getting to say the prayer I wanted to say. I had to concentrate to get my mouth to make the words. It was like I could hear them in my head, but something was stopping me from forming them.

'And I felt threatened, like something was trying to force me to stop. I was actually quite scared of what would happen. I could feel something surrounding me. I guess it felt like it would attack if it could, but as long as I kept saying the words, it couldn't. But saying the words was so hard.

'With hindsight, I think that there was a fight-back on that landing. I was aware of an anger, rage even. Mostly I just get aware of whatever it is, but no real fight. The house is free of problems now, anyway.'

Canon Michael Wadsworth recalls going with another priest to help a colleague suffering psychic persecution in his own vicarage.

'Ornaments – some quite heavy – were moving, often in the middle of the night. He was distraught – at the end of his tether. There was definitely a malign influence – a troubled spirit.

'We conducted a Requiem Eucharist and opened every window and every door – it was a fine summer's day. While we worked inside the house, he went outside and shouted at the top of his voice, "Do your bloody worst!"'

Apparently, it worked.

What was perhaps Michael Wadsworth's most curious case involved a very old prayer book given as a legacy to his church. It had belonged to a priest and went into general use.

'It was interesting how, in at least two homes belonging to people who attended the church and used that particular prayer book, things started to happen – poltergeist phenomena and voices. I didn't tell people, just ceased to use the prayer book and blessed it, privately. And it stopped.

'I'm probably being whimsical about it, but being in my job makes you like this. I've come away with the lifetime motto: there's no such thing as a gratuitous coincidence. Sometimes it seems as if we're trembling on the brink of the absurd, but religion is like that.'

If all this has made it seem relatively easy – a splash of holy water, a well-timed ritual and, even if there's a struggle, the good guys always win – it's important to point out that it *doesn't* always work. Most deliverance ministers have painful ongoing cases they can't discuss because the victims would be identified.

There are apparent presences which repeated Requiem Eucharists have failed to erase. There are cases where parish priests have suffered breakdowns or even quit the ministry. Most deliverance ministers will tell you they've watched objects move or at least felt the intense cold, a cold you experience inside as a kind of frigid void. The borderline between psychiatric illness and what one senior exorcist calls psychic or demonic *oppression* is continually blurred.

In *Midwinter of the Spirit*, a new Bishop of Hereford, having heard of Merrily's problems in *The Wine of Angels*, invites her to take on the additional job of deliverance consultant for the diocese.

Consultant is an appropriate word, as the diocesan exorcist is mostly there to advise. If you have a problem, you normally take it to the local vicar or rector who may then refer it to the deliverance minister.

Which is what I did, approaching the then deliverance minister for Hereford to ask him what kind of a job he thought this would be for a woman.

'A very dangerous one,' he said.

3 MIDWINTER

Under the window, a fourteenth-century bishop slept on, his marble mitre like a nightcap. But the tomb of his saintly predecessor, Thomas Cantilupe, was in pieces – stone sections laid out, Merrily thought, like a display of postmodern garden ornaments.

Midwinter of the Spirit

MIDWINTER ENTERS the old city of Hereford, its Cathedral, its secret history. The deliverance consultant is appointed by the Bishop, who must approve any major exorcism. To put Merrily right at the heart of things, I gave her an office at the Cathedral and a time-share in the Bishop's lay-secretary, Sophie Hill, a smart, elegant, slightly severe woman who 'works for the Cathedral'.

The Cathedral gatehouse, Hereford

Sophie's office, and Merrily's deliverance base in Hereford, is above the gatehouse, overlooking Broad Street and the cathedral green. Across the road in Gwynne Street, is the home of the former diocesan exorcist, Canon Thomas Dobbs, a man bitterly opposed to the idea of a woman deliverance consultant, pointing out that 'the first exorcist was Jesus Christ'. Dobbs is determined that Merrily should be exposed to deliverance at its most disturbing.

Hereford Cathedral and the Bishops Palace across the Wye

As *Midwinter* opens, she's learning about the rules and techniques of exorcism in a remote part of the Brecon Beacons, where the SAS do their training (and where exorcism *is* taught). The course leader and Merrily's spiritual director is the Revd Huw Owen, blunt, cynical but far from sceptical. The danger of being a woman exorcist? Huw doesn't dress it up.

> ... headlights floated down the valley, a long way away. She thought of Jane back home in Ledwardine and felt isolated, cut off. A night breeze razored down from crags she could no longer see.
> 'Listen,' Huw said, 'the ordination of women is indisputably the most titillating development in the Church since the Reformation. They'll follow you home, they'll breathe into your phone at night, break into your vestry and tamper with your gear. Crouch in the back pews and masturbate through your sermons ... prime target for every psychotic grinder of the dark satanic mills that ever sacrificed a chicken ...'

Merrily's first assignment takes her to the old Hereford General Hospital, once the city's lunatic asylum, where she encounters a patient who makes even seasoned nurses nervous. This incident is based almost entirely on a story I was told by a local former nursing sister.

Victoria suspension bridge over the Wye, Hereford

Fairly soon, a body is recovered from the River Wye near Victoria Bridge, not far from the old hospital and the story switches to Dinedor Hill and the Cathedral and the ancient church of St Cosmas and St Damian, by way of the Dinedor ley and the legacy of —

Alfred Watkins

You won't find an official monument to Alfred Watkins in Hereford – an almost criminal omission. There used to be a short footpath by the side of Tesco called Watkins Way, but even that disappeared. All that remains is the plaque on his former house near the Cathedral.

Watkins was a county councillor, a magistrate, a brewer, a pioneer photographer, an archaeologist and, for thousands of people all over the world, the most important Herefordian in history. For this was the man who discovered ley lines.

OK, *I* don't know whether or not leys exist. All I know is that the *idea* of them changed the way I look at a landscape, gave me a feel for patterns of hills and meadows, mounds and churches that I never had before. Or maybe, subliminally, I did. Maybe we all do; whatever, Alfred Watkins' contribution to our perception of Britain is unique.

Sketch map of the ley line running between Dinedor Camp and the church of St Cosmos and St Damian at Stretford

A ley is a – usually invisible – line which Watkins believed linked ancient monuments. He worked out that many Bronze Age ritual sites – standing stones, stone circles, burial mounds – had been arranged to follow straight lines across the countryside. As many medieval and pre-medieval churches were built on sites of earlier worship and castle mottes were sometimes formed around burial mounds, they would also sometimes occur on straight lines. Watkins presented his theories to the Woolhope Naturalists' Field Club which, of course, still exists, and published them in *Early British Trackways* and his most celebrated work, *The Old Straight Track*, a book which continues to change lives.

Alfred Watkins' original research was conducted on maps and on foot. If you stand on the edge of the Iron Age camp on Dinedor Hill and look across the city you can actually see one of his most famous leys. Stand where you can align the Cathedral tower with the spire of All Saints and you're on it.

What does this mean?

Watkins was a little cagey about it. He rarely went further than the suggestion that leys were ancient trackways, possible trading routes. But when you read between the lines of *The Old Straight Track* it's clear that he was sensing a greater mystery.

It was left to a succession of later writers to develop the more seductive

Left: Church Street, Hereford. Right: Alfred Watkins' house, The Vineyard, Hereford

theories. The occultist Dion Fortune was the first to suggest, in her novel *The Goatfoot God*, that Watkins' leys might be channels of psychic energy, a theory adopted by dowsers, who began to track the lines with rods and pendulums, and developed by John Michell in his seminal book, *The View over Atlantis*.

The latest theory, promoted by the writer Paul Devereux and others, is that leys were 'spirit roads', routes along which the dead were believed to walk and where tribal shamans sought communication with them. Supporting evidence for this includes the tradition of 'coffin paths' – established routes by which the dead were taken into country churches, seen as memories of leys – and, of course, the tendency for ghost sightings to be reported on leys.

The narrow Church Street, or Capuchin Way, which links Hereford Cathedral with High Town follows one of Watkins' leys. This is where Merrily's friend, Lol Robinson lives in *Midwinter of the Spirit*.

But the Dinedor ley, passing through the centre of the city and the Cathedral itself, is central to the plot ... and one of the few it's possible to see almost from beginning to end.

Dinedor Hill

— is often said to be Hereford's mother hill. This may be where the city began, as an Iron Age camp, the ramparts of which can still be seen in the shade of mature trees at the top of the hill.

Although the name Dinedor comes from the ancient British or Welsh *dyn*, meaning fort, the earthworks on the hill suggest a community rather than a military base, and the idea of an earlier ritual site on the hill has been strengthened by the recent discovery of the Dinedor Serpent or Rotherwas Ribbon, of which more later.

If we follow the line to Hereford Cathedral we encounter the shrine of —

Dinedor Hillfort, four miles to the south of Hereford

St Thomas Cantilupe

This shrine was probably second only to Thomas Becket's in Canterbury Cathedral as a centre of healing. Candles may still be lit at the refurbished tomb standing in the north transept.

Born around 1218, Tommy Canty, as he's affectionately known to Merrily's spiritual director, Huw Owen, was the most celebrated medieval Bishop of Hereford, a man revered in his lifetime who, it was said, could bring little birds to the window when he celebrated mass. An experienced lawyer, he was appointed Bishop of Hereford in 1275, in the reign of Edward I. In a dispute with the Archbishop of Canterbury, Thomas was excommunicated, went to Rome to appeal to the Pope and died of a fever. His body was boiled to remove the flesh and his bones brought back to Hereford, where they were entombed, originally in the Lady Chapel before a new shrine was built in the north transept in 1287.

Cantilupe Shrine, Hereford Cathedral

By this time, miracles were being reported, beginning with the calming of a Hereford ironmonger's wife who, possibly because of a drink problem, attacked her husband, bit her mother and harangued God and the neighbours. She claimed to have a vision of 'Saint' Thomas, although he wouldn't be canonised until 1320.

In the region of 500 miraculous cures were claimed over the next 25 years, with pilgrims being carried into the Cathedral on stretchers and walking out. People too ill to be carried to the Cathedral were measured in string which was then used as the wick of a candle dedicated to St Thomas. Animals, too, were cured.

Around the time *Midwinter* was taking shape, the tomb was dismantled for cleaning, repair and refurbishment, for the first time since 1860 when, I was told, something very disturbing was found inside. Not this time, however.

As far as I know.

Left: Carving at All Saints, Hereford. Right: Sheelagh-na-gig corbel, Kilpeck church

ALL SAINTS CHURCH, HEREFORD

— is the next point on the ley.

With its flourishing café, All Saints on a weekday has a real feel of what you imagine a church would have been like in medieval times, the vibrant centre of a community. It also has a ghost who likes to sit near the organ. And, talking of organs, in the café area upstairs there's a carving which suggests a male sheelagh-na-gig ... a rampant little figure linked to fertility.

The healing theme of the Dinedor ley is picked up again at its final point.

THE CHURCH OF ST COSMAS AND ST DAMIAN

This mysterious little double-naved church in the hamlet of Stretford, near Dilwyn, is dedicated to two fourth-century saints linked with physicians and surgeons and, although made redundant in 1969, was used until quite recently for an annual thanksgiving service for doctors and nurses.

A healing well is said to have disappeared from the church precincts, although many people still regard it as a centre of healing, and ley-hunters have pointed to some old stones in the raised churchyard as evidence of pagan worship. However, when we visited the church in March 2007 for a TV programme which, in the

Opposite: All Saints Church, Hereford

end, was never made, archaeologist Jodie Lewis suggested the stones might actually be the remains of the holy well.

St Cosmas and St Damian has been maintained by the Churches Conservation Trust, remains consecrated, and occasional services are still held there ...

... unlike some churches along the Border which have fallen into disuse and, in a few cases, into ruins. Reverting, some would say, to their ancient origins as circles of stone ...

The Church of St Cosmas and St Damian, Stretford

4 WITCHLIGHTS

Curtains of cold, red light hung from the heavens into the roofless nave. When Robin emerged from the tower, she took his cold hand in her even colder ones. The church was mournful around her.

A Crown of Lights

Now it's coming up to Candlemas, or *Imbolc*, the old Celtic festival of the first light, celebrated in early February, and we slip into mid-Wales, directly into the path of —

THE DRAGON

There are five medieval churches in and around Radnor Forest, all dedicated to St Michael, the archangel responsible for dealing with dragons.

We lived in Radnor for over 15 years, and although I never actually saw a dragon I did once photograph what ghost-hunters like to call 'an orb' and ufologists like to call, um, a UFO, over Castell Crugeryr, a very prominent castle mound off an elbow of road near Fforest Inn.

Castell Crugeryr in snow

Tomen Castle on the lower slopes of Radnor Forest

The Four Stones near Kinnerton

Discoed Church and its yew tree

It's an odd place, Radnor Forest. Not a forest in the accepted sense, as it actually has comparatively few trees. Forest, traditionally, was just a term for a hunting ground. This is an area of wild green hills, and the smallest hills are the castle mounds, several – Castell Crugeryr, Tomen Castle, New Radnor Castle, Hundred House Mount – visible from the country lanes known as the A44 and A481 which slither across it.

The Forest also has some nicely-obscure prehistoric stones – notably the Four Stones near Kinnerton, which appear in the third Merrily novel, *A Crown of Lights*.

Behind a hedge, this is a safe, almost cosy site from which to contemplate the quarry-savaged skyline and the lofty Old Radnor church to the west.

Old Radnor, dominant though it appears, is not one of the five St Michael churches which form a slightly squashed pentagram across the hills, extending from Cefnllys – lovely spot – near Llandrindod Wells, up to Llanfihangel Rhydithon, down to Llanfihangel-nant-Melan, Cascob and finally Discoed with its venerable yew tree, close to the English border.

Llandegley Rocks – the Dragon's Back

A stretch of hillside near Llandegley, in the Forest, is still known as The Dragon's Back, and a former clergyman at Llanfihangel Rhydithon wrote,

> I often spoke to an old man who lived up on the slopes of the Forest and maintained that though he had never seen it he had heard it breathing.
> Was it because of the dragon that our Christian ancestors ringed it around with St Michael churches ...?

Several sources suggest that Radnor Forest was particularly vulnerable to the forces of darkness and required protection at the highest level. One legend warns that if any of the churches is allowed to close, the evil will return.

But what was meant by evil?

Is the dragon simply a symbol of the ancient pagan religions represented by the standing stones, circles and mounds all over Radnor Forest? (As *A Crown of Lights* was being written, archaeologists were documenting the discovery of a massive henge in the Radnor Valley, not far from the location of the novel's one invented village, Old Hindwell.) Or was there believed to be a real and active evil which could be repelled only by a combination of old and new religion?

The Charms

The idea for *A Crown of Lights* began to ferment when a member of an old Radnorshire family, Glyn Morgan, sent me a copy of a charm found in a farmhouse in north Radnorshire invoking holy names to protect the farmer, his horses, cows, sheep, pigs and poultry from molestation, witches' spells and the power of Satan.

Its mixture of Christianity and paganism was remarkably similar to a well-known exorcism which you can still see on a wall of the most remote of the St Michael churches at Cascob. Dating back to around 1700, it's known as the Abracadabra Charm because of its traditional use of a magic word since devalued by generations of stage magicians.

```
ABRACADABRA
 ABRACADAB
  ABRACAD
   ABRAC
    ABR
     A
```

In the name of the Father, son and the Holy Ghost Amen x x x and in the name of the Lord Jesus Christ I will deliver Elizabeth Loyd from all witchcraft and from all Evil spirites & from all evil men or Women or Wizardes or hardness of hart Amen x x x

So was there, in Radnor Forest, a hybrid religion, a form of semi-pagan hedge-Christianity, and what remains of it today?

Cascob Church

In *A Crown of Lights*, a pagan couple move into a farmhouse and are presented by 'the local people' with a copy of a similar protective charm, before becoming the target of what is effectively a witch-hunt led by a fundamentalist Anglican priest with a few secrets of his own.

The farmhouse happens to have, on its land, a ruined church, which forms part of the protective pentagram of St Michael churches. To avoid ruining the reputation of an existing ruined church, I had to invent one. However, there is one in Radnor Forest, Ednol, of which rather less remains than the church at Old Hindwell. There are also a couple of ruins in Herefordshire which fit the image. The first is at Llanwarne, a few miles from Ross-on-Wye. And the other – which also serves as an introduction to the Frome Valley, location of the next chapter – illustrates another aspect of exorcism.

Avenbury Church

The remains of St Mary's, Avenbury, lie in a shallow grave of tangled woodland, enclosed by tall trees, embalmed by creepers. Mentioned in the Domesday Book of 1086, the church was decommissioned by the diocese in 1946 ... and if you're alone here at dusk, just be grateful for the silence.

The ghost stories have been circulating for at least 50 years. It's said that a church organ sometimes moans at close of day. That bells peal in the roofless tower. That a company of cowled monks still sings in the opened shell of the nave.

'No, I don't particularly like the place,' the Revd Graham Sykes says carefully. 'It makes me feel uneasy.'

Graham, vicar of Bromyard in East Herefordshire, is responsible for the former parish of Avenbury where this church was left to rot. It might be a thousand years old, but it was never an architectural treasure. Another local vicar has visited it just once and has no plans to return.

'It's a horrible place. It just *feels* horrible. I've never been anywhere before where I've felt so much ... badness.'

But it's not the ghostly monks that offend the local clergy, or the spooky soundtrack. It's the fact that St Mary's still seems to be a place of worship.

The wrong kind, of course. Like many medieval churches, it's believed to occupy a place of pre-Christian sanctity, and its absentee owner actually erected a sign identifying it as an 'ancient pagan site'. So now, as its stonework crumbles, St Mary's has become fully available, day and night, for ... well, for anything you fancy, basically.

Amongst the rubble below the tower's last remaining rafter, I found signs of a recent fire and the remains of candles burned on the broken graves of local

Above: the site of Ednol Church. Below: the ruins of Avenbury Church (left) and Llanwarne Church (right)

families. The suspicion, naturally, is of black magic rites or at least occult games involving teenagers attracted by the church's sinister reputation and its isolation.

'I do think places are affected by the things that happen in them,' Graham Sykes says. 'I think kids have been going out there, maybe at night, for a laugh.'

But when the laughter dies and they go home alone, perhaps wondering what they might have disturbed ... that's often when the problems begin.

As recently as last year, a small outbreak of apparent poltergeist phenomena was reported at homes in the area – moving objects, footsteps heard overhead, cold spots. Several of these cases were said to have involved families known to be fascinated by the ruins of St Mary's Church. The talk was of ouija-board experiments – attempts to contact the unquiet dead of Avenbury.

As the building isn't theirs any more, there's nothing the Church can do about whatever goes on there. Besides, paganism is an accepted faith and these days even satanists are likely to claim their religious rights. Christian clergy can only address what they perceive to be the spiritual or psychological effects of what may or may not be happening.

'I think,' Graham Sykes says, 'that if people dabble with the occult then it affects them – disturbs their psyche. And it can manifest in psycho-kinetic energy. I think they're playing with fire.'

Graham remains unconvinced by the old ghost-stories at Avenbury, suggesting its bad atmosphere may have more to do with what's been happening there since it became known as a haunted ruin.

'I think that it's been spiritually damaged by people playing around ... and *that's* why it's an uneasy place. Some places do need to be healed. But first, the people need to be healed.'

Which brings us to *The Cure of Souls*.

5   Lady of the Bines

A second black pole appeared, rearing hard against the northern sky, and this one had a short crosspiece like – his first thought – a gibbet. From it hung something limp and shrivelled, the skeletal spine of a dead garland; when he passed between the two poles his bare elbow brushed against the remains with a dry, papery crackle. Now he could see the extent of it: dozens of black poles against the pale night, in lines to either side of him across the barren ground ... like a site laid out for a mass-crucifixion.

The Cure of Souls

So where do you get your ideas?

As this is acknowledged worldwide as the most blindingly obvious question aimed at novelists, you'd think people would be embarrassed to ask it by now. But they aren't, and I actually have an answer, apart from the one that goes, 'I buy them at night off this guy in dark glasses and a hoodie on the edge of the Plascarreg Estate.'

The simple answer is: they come out of the location. You find a place that looks interesting, examine its history, ancient and recent, and its folklore, look at its current preoccupations, stir them all together and add a crime. That's it, really.

The Cure of Souls is set in the Frome Valley of eastern Herefordshire. Not the most widely known area of the county. Places quite near to an established tourist area seldom are, and the Frome Valley will always be in the shadow of the Malverns. Its hills are discreet and its river is usually unobtrusive. As Lol Robinson sings,

Looking across the Frome Valley to the Malvern Hills

> *The River Frome goes nowhere in particular*
> *It isn't very wide*
> *There's nothing on the other side.*

Actually, Lol may have been using the Frome Valley as a metaphor for the condition of his life at the time. As the novel opens, he's working in the (fictional) village of Knight's Frome – not far from Bishop's Frome and Canon Frome – as assistant to Prof. Levin, the music producer, now assembling his own recording studio there.

Nearby is a converted hop kiln. Not unusual in the Frome Valley, where very few hop kilns these days are used for the hops which were once, thanks to its lush, deep soil, the valley's biggest industry.

Hops

— put the flavour in beer. They are related to nettles and cannabis. The hop plant climbs clockwise around its pole and can reach 20 feet, dying back to the soil every winter. After picking – a major operation – they are dried in hop kilns, which pierce the skyline across the Frome and Lugg Valleys.

It was an intoxicatingly mysterious world, full of arcane terms like hop-crib and hop-devil, and the smell of sulphur. But now, thanks to cheap hops from Off, the Herefordshire industry is in serious decline. Many hop-yards have fallen into dereliction. And a derelict hop-yard is a spooky place, as Lol discovers in *The Cure of Souls*.

Top: the Frome valley with hop-yards. Bottom: hop kilns for drying hops

Before cheap hops from Off, the biggest scourge was the voracious Verticillium Wilt, which would put acres of hop-yard into quarantine, symbolised in the novel by The Lady of the Bines, a spectral figure haunting hop-yards. If you see her, your crop is doomed.

Just as strawberries in the polytunnels further west are now picked mainly by East Europeans, the hops used to be picked by incoming seasonal labour, the Valleys people from South Wales, the Dudleys from the Black Country and – most interesting, as far as this novel is concerned, the gypsies – mainly —

Romanies

'Romanies respect, sometimes consult, the ancestors, but they let the dead lie. Don't ever trust the dead. We have a word ... *mulo* ... the Romani word for a ghost. This word is also used for a vampire. The living dead.

We don't worry about your dead – we'll settle down to sleep in your cemeteries any night of the week. We believe that the Romani dead ... they don't come back for no reason. We're very afraid of the vengeful power of our dead.'

Opposite: a modern hop-yard; above: hop picking by hand (twentieth century)

Hop picking by hand (twentieth century)

This is Al Boswell talking. In the novel, Al is the Romani craftsman behind the famous Boswell Guitar – known these days, thanks to modern marketing, as *The Lute of the Frome*. This much-prized instrument is fashioned from a carefully chosen mixture of woods, which are taken sparingly without the destruction of a single tree. The philosophy of 'borrowing the earth' was borrowed from Patrick Jasper Lee's book, which explains the methods of the *Chovihano*, or Romani shaman. I learned a lot from this book and others possibly out of print now.

For example … a Romani ghost may appear not at dead of night, but dead of noon. In the brightest sunlight, *the time of no shadows*. A nice twist.

I promise there are no vampires in this book. But *The Cure of Souls* does deal with some of the central problems of deliverance: when to exorcise and how far to go, with the atmosphere of a converted hop kiln apparently disturbed as a result of a murder committed there.

Just occasionally a novel happens the other way round, starting not with location but with murder. If it's real murder you're on dangerous ground.

6 A Dark Lamp

Fred's leaning across, apologising to Rose. 'Now I know you won't mind, my love, but we gotter drop Jane off in Ledwardine ...'
The Lamp of the Wicked

In this scene, Merrily is dreaming, and it's not the kind of dream anyone needs. But the nightmare grin of the goblinesque mass-murderer Fred West seems destined to become an image out of folklore, swimming up from the darkest undercurrent in rural Herefordshire.

The scale of Fred's evil may never be fully known, the investigation having ended – arguably because of the cost – rather prematurely in my view. But then, what do I know?

More than I feel comfortable with, to be honest. When I first thought of the theme of *The Lamp of the Wicked*, my wife urged me to leave it alone. It was all too recent, the pain too close to the surface.

Fred West was found hanged in his cell before he could stand trial for the murders of women and girls at the home he shared with his wife Rosemary in Cromwell Street, Gloucester. Rose is now serving life for her part in the murders. Fred was a builder and knew how to dispose of bodies under concrete. As a result there were lots of black jokes about patios – the British way of dealing with it.

But, in the end, it was never really dealt with to anyone's satisfaction and its aftermath still hangs like noxious industrial smoke over Gloucester, Herefordshire and the Forest of Dean.

And I kept running into people connected with the case or the West family.

A neighbour of ours recalled some amusing but, with hindsight, slightly sinister stories about a relative of Fred who, apparently, had once worked ... well, very close to where we live. Geoffrey Wansell, who wrote (very much against the clock, so that it could hit the shelves in the wake of Rose's trial) the first and most explicit West biography, *An Evil Love*, would tell me how, after listening to the tapes of Fred's interrogation by police, he would go into the church near his home to try and remove the aura of raw evil they always left behind. Gordon Burn, author of the devastating *Happy like Murderers*, told me he never wanted to deal with a subject this dark again, ever.

But Prof. Bernard Knight, the pathologist who conducted autopsies on several of the victims, pointed out that aspects of the case were still ... unresolved.

Kempley Church chancel arch and chancel

The implications were extremely sinister, and I decided to go ahead.

Fiction can often say more than speculative non-fiction, but this is the darkest in the series and some readers prefer to avoid it. Personally, I don't think that what the Wests did should ever be forgotten, if only because there's a lot more that needs to come out.

Fred West was born in Much Marcle where, after his arrest, bodies were discovered in Fingerpost field – a lovely spot, actually, not far from the idyllic Kempley Church with its medieval murals. Because he ended up in Gloucester, Fred is usually seen as a low-life city boy; in fact, he was very much a Welsh Border man: practical, independent, self-sufficient. He killed out of expediency and always (to use building trade terminology) 'made good' afterwards.

However, I was determined that *The Lamp of the Wicked* should deal less with the sickening reality of life in Cromwell Street than with the emotional aftermath over a very wide area of western Britain. There are dozens of parents, siblings and boyfriends of missing girls who, not least because the case was too rapidly closed,

Opposite: details of the Romanesque wall paintings in Kempley Church

will never know if they were victims of Fred and Rose. Most people connected with the case believe that many more victims – 40 is one informed estimate – may be lying in their unmarked graves.

Lamp is about a man apparently influenced, several years later, by the West murders. It's not, I hope, a gruesome or a sadistic novel as much as an emotional one. But it is dark, and it would have been unfair to burden Much Marcle with a fictional development of the West legend, so I switched the scene to nearby Ross-on-Wye, and the Coughton Valley. Because of the nature of the plot it was necessary to create a new village, Underhowle, named after nearby Howle Hill. However, this is still very much a real area, just a few miles from Symonds Yat, which was already linked with a murder by a man known as Black Dai, a Fred West copycat killer from South Wales.

Lamp also deals with the health-damaging, mind-altering effects of living under high-voltage power lines. Massive pylons carrying power to Gloucestershire stalk the Coughton Valley, and I was interested in a theory that linked electricity to so-called alien abduction. In the novel, an environmental activist sees an invisible invasion.

Pylons crossing the Coughton Valley

A DARK LAMP 49

'If we could see all the TV and satellite signals, all the radio waves serving mobile phones, police communications, cab fleets, air networks, the sky would be this kind of poisonous black the whole day long. If we could smell them like exhaust fumes we'd all choke to death. But it's a whole lot more subtle than that. They zip unseen and unfelt through our atmosphere and our bodies and our brains ... the insidious wind that blows through us all ... flesh and tissue and bones ...'

The novel also recalls the plague that settled in Ross in 1637, with major loss of life and the town in quarantine, details of which can be found in *The Story of Ross* by Pat Hughes and Heather Hurley. They note a report by Thomas Jenkins recalling:

The dead were buried at night in their wearing apparel in deep graves or pits, numbers at a time ... The bodies were brought in carts and slipped out of the carts into the grave. Good old Vicar Price used to stand on the cross solemnising the funerals by torchlight.

Later, the minister, Philip Price, led the townsfolk through the streets at 5 a.m. 'chanting a litany with supplications for deliverance', after which the plague is said to have abated.

Ross-on-Wye: St Mary's Church and the Plague Cross

Clockwise from top: (Ross) Wye Street; the Man of Ross; gazebo tower and the old lock-up

This is echoed in *The Lamp of the Wicked*, in which the disposal of bodies by night is a recurrent issue. On a less-infected level, the novel also looks at evidence of the Roman town of —

Ariconium

which, as local historian Brian Cave wrote, 'remains as a ghost. Though gone in body, its spirit still marks itself upon the landscape.'

Cave thought Ariconium, around what is now Weston under Penyard, near Ross, may have been built to house Roman garrisons protecting iron mines in the nearby Forest of Dean.

You can find it along the old Roman road to Gloucester. Just follow the pylons.

The Forest of Dean

7 A Real Creeper

'Mr Holmes, they were the footprints of a gigantic hound.'
But where were they actually planted? On Dartmoor ... or the Welsh Border?

It's over 50 years since Maurice Campbell, chairman at the time of the Sherlock Holmes Society, published a controversial pamphlet, *The Hound of the Baskervilles: Dartmoor or Herefordshire?*

Today, the Sherlock Holmes Society is in no doubt: it's Dartmoor. But the Arthur Conan Doyle Society tends to disagree. The evidence for the spectral Hound having a paw either side of the Border, between Kington and Clyro, is considerable and was explored in the sixth Merrily Watkins book, *The Prayer of the Night Shepherd*. In this novel, a hard-up hotelier, like many before him, is attempting to build a future around the most famous of all Sherlock Holmes stories.

The unnamed Night Shepherd makes a brief appearance in the Baskerville Manuscript shown to Holmes before he comes to the aid of Sir Henry Baskerville, a man who seems to have inherited a curse. In the Manuscript, it's the Night Shepherd who directs friends of the unpleasant Sir Hugo Baskerville to the spot where he's having his throat torn out.

But who directed Sir Arthur Conan Doyle to the Hound?

'I have the idea of a real creeper for the *Strand*,' Conan Doyle wrote in 1901 to Greenough Smith, editor of the London magazine that would print Sherlock Holmes stories ahead of their publication in book form.

There was one stipulation, however, Doyle said. 'I must do it with my friend Fletcher Robinson.'

Robinson, much younger, at 28, than Doyle, and from Devon, had entertained the great man, during a golfing holiday in Norfolk, with the legend of a spectral hound. Doyle was inspired.

So which legend *was* this? As far as the Holmes Society was concerned, it had to be the story of Sir Richard Cabell, the most hated man on Dartmoor, and his revenant canine companion. When Doyle and Robinson went to Devon to research the novel, the coachman who drove them around was one Harry Baskerville.

Case closed? Apparently not. The most recent Conan Doyle biography, *Teller of Tales* by Daniel Stashower, points out that Greenough Smith later recalled Robinson saying he'd found the legend in 'a Welsh guide book'. And the proposed title of the book was disclosed by Conan Doyle in a letter to his mother in Scotland before he and Robinson had been to Dartmoor or, presumably, met Harry Baskerville.

However, Welsh and Herefordshire guidebooks, to this day, often retell the story of —

BLACK VAUGHAN OF HERGEST

Hergest Court should not be confused with Hergest Croft, where the gardens are open to the public. Hergest Court, a much bleaker-looking place in a more exposed location, doesn't do gardens.

I first went there in the late 1980s to record a programme for BBC Radio Wales. The tenant farmer at the time, John Williams, remembered the 'prickly feeling'

Hergest Court

Kington Church

that went up his back when he once heard, from the hall, what sounded like the patter of huge paws in an upstairs room. Later, he said, he saw a hound-like shadow passing in front of him towards the inner hall.

You'll still find people in Kington who won't go down the lane to Hergest after dark. Bob Jenkins, journalist, historian and Kington oracle, told me about a man cycling to work at Kington Camp during the Second World War.

> 'Near Hergest Court, he saw this enormous hound which he'd never seen before and never saw again. The hound had huge eyes – that's what impressed him. He had a feeling that there was something that just wasn't real about it.'

To this day, you can hear accounts of psychic disturbance at Hergest Court, and it all seems to be down to Black Vaughan – Thomas Vaughan, who lived at the Court when it was much bigger and more fortified than the present sawn-off farmhouse.

The events in the Baskerville Manuscript take place during The Great Rebellion, the English Civil War. Black Vaughan – so called, apparently, merely because of the colour of his hair – took part in the previous civil conflict, the Wars of the Roses. Vaughan changed sides, from Lancaster to York (changing sides comes easily to

The Vaughan tomb, Kington Church

border people; it's about survival) and was said to have been killed at a battle near Banbury. His headless body was brought back to Kington, to be buried next to his wife Ellen Gethin ('the terrible'), who has her own legend. They now lie side by side in a rather spooky tomb in the Vaughan Chapel in Kington Parish Church.

Vaughan has been described as a notorious tyrant, although there's nothing in history to support this. It was only after death that he began to measure up to Hugo Baskerville's level of infamy, when a spectral hound was also seen, its appearances heralding death in the Vaughan family. The ghost of Vaughan himself began to exhibit signs of revenant-rage, rampaging through Kington, turning over farmers' carts and disrupting church services by manifesting as a bull. Fairly soon, nobody wanted to come to Kington Market and the town's economy began to suffer.

It was decided, at this stage, that Vaughan needed to be properly exorcised.

This was a big job that took 12 priests. Ella Mary Leather's *The Folk-lore of Herefordshire* tells how Vaughan appeared during the ritual, insisting he had now become a devil. Eventually subdued, after a lot of shouting and extinguishing of candles, his spirit was shrunk, confined to a snuff box – local historian Alan Lloyd suggests this was actually a candle-snuffer box – and buried under a stone at the bottom of the pool in front of Hergest Court.

Only the Hound remained, as a harbinger of death in the Vaughan family and a spectral watchdog around Hergest, where no Vaughan has resided since the death of the Revd Silvanus Vaughan in 1706.

THE FINAL PROBLEM

So is it Dartmoor or the Welsh Border?

I think Conan Doyle's hound is a mongrel. This is what novelists do – pinch material from different sources, muddying its origins. But, as far as the hound's pedigree goes, the balance of probability falls towards the Border.

The original Baskervilles were Norman barons who came over after the Conquest, building castles at Eardisley in Herefordshire and Aberedw across the border in Radnorshire. Their descendants owned the mansion Clyro Court, now the Baskerville Hall Hotel. The pub in the village of Clyro has always been The Baskerville Arms. If you look at the family tree of the Vaughans of Hergest you'll find evidence of inter-marriage with the Baskervilles of Clyro.

After publication of *The Prayer of the Night Shepherd* raked up the embers of the old argument and a story in the *Daily Telegraph* had Hound fans snapping at each other in the paper's letters column, I had an email from Christopher Roden, of the Arthur Conan Doyle Society, who explained,

> Conan Doyle's first wife, Louise, whom he married in 1885, was one of the Hawkins of Minsterworth family. When he married her, and until her death, Louise was receiving an annuity from her brother Joseph's farms, the Bettws and Whitehall farms at Clyro. A neighbouring owner was Thomas Baskerville Mynors Baskerville, and the Hawkins farms were eventually sold to Ralph Hopton Baskerville in 1907, following Louise's death in 1906.

It's inconceivable, given such a close connection, that Conan Doyle wouldn't have visited the area at some stage.

It seems to be quite impossible that ACD would not have known the legend of Black Vaughan's demon dog.

Vaughans also married Hawkinses.

Around the same time, the late Geoffrey Hopton, last of the Hopton/Baskervilles in Clyro, told me that his grandmother's understanding of the situation had been that Conan Doyle did indeed know about Black Vaughan and had asked if he could use the name Baskerville in his novel, as it had more resonance. The Baskervilles said yes ... as long as he located the novel somewhere else.

This was confirmed in *Out of the Shadows: The Untold Story of Conan Doyle's First Family*, by a descendant, Georgina Doyle.

The final evidence, for me, is the coincidence of names. Apart from Baskerville itself, there's Mortimer – it's Dr Mortimer who first brings the problem to the attention of Sherlock Holmes. The Mortimers, of course, were for many years the most powerful Norman family in the Welsh Marches.

There's also Stapleton, the naturalist, a key character in the novel and the name of a hamlet just beyond Presteigne, a few miles from Kington.

So where's Baskerville Hall?

Although there's evidence in the cellars of an earlier building on the site, Clyro Court, former home of the Baskervilles, now the Baskerville Hall Hotel, is Victorian and therefore unlikely to be Conan Doyle's model. It could be that Baskerville Hall is on Dartmoor, but if you're looking for a Welsh Border house which fits the image, it's worth investigating —

Kinnersley Castle

This Welsh border stronghold, a few miles from Clyro on the Herefordshire side, was held for generations by the de la Bere family, two generations of whom are entombed in the Church of St Cosmas and St Damian at Stretford.

Kinnersley Castle

But in the mid sixteenth century it became the property of Roger Vaughan, MP for Radnorshire, and grandson of Black Vaughan himself, who spent a fortune turning a Norman castle into a state-of-the-art Tudor mansion, with tall leaded windows and a four-storey central tower.

If you want to feel the power of the Vaughans, this is the place. Over a fireplace is the emblem of the Vaughans, a child with a snake wound around his neck (it's been speculated that this is what gave Conan Doyle the idea for *The Speckled Band*, the one where ... well, I won't spoil it if you haven't read it). And there's a ceiling with the heads of hounds, dragons and a green man.

There are yew trees outside, close to the castle. There may have been, as at Baskerville Hall, a yew alley ...

It doesn't end ...

In 1987, Jenny Vaughan, a businesswoman from the Midlands, came to Kington with a friend to investigate her family history. She didn't, fortunately perhaps, see the hound. But she did see a bull in the church where, you'll remember, the angry spirit of Black Vaughan was said to take taurine form. I talked to Jenny, for radio, inside the church, some months later. It made very convincing radio.

> The inside of his nostrils – this was one of the most vivid things – were very, very red, like a racehorse when it's just stopped running. And it was wet. It was dripping moisture or something on to the ground. It was as though it was hanging in strings ... I'm a hard-headed business person but I can't deny it. I've seen it.

Over at Hergest Court, the hauntings, it seems, have never gone away. Tenants regularly report disturbances.

As for Hergest pool, where the spirit of Black Vaughan is supposed to lie in its snuff box, Roy Palmer records in his *Herefordshire Folklore* that when there were attempts to fill in the pool some years ago the project was abandoned after the water began to bubble ominously.

A few years ago, when the water level dropped, it was decided the pool should be cleaned out, and a large stone became visible. Historian Alan Lloyd thought this might be a good opportunity to find out if there was any kind of container underneath it and tried to persuade local farmers with mechanical diggers to check it out.

Nobody was prepared to go near. I don't even think Gomer Parry would've done it.

STANNER ROCKS

Much of the action in *Prayer* takes place at the Stanner Hall Hotel, close to Stanner Rocks, said to be the oldest rocks (over 700 million years old) in Wales.

The rocks can be seen from the edge of the Kington bypass on the Welsh side, bulging out of the hillside foliage like Stone Age sculpture. A combination of geography and air currents means that some spots up there have an almost Mediterranean climate, and Fred Slater, in *The Nature of Central Wales*, describes the rocks as a 'botanical jewel,' because of the rare – and even unique – plant species found there.

As for the Stanner Hall Hotel ... that's roughly in the vicinity of the less decrepit Dunfield Manor, now a conference centre. Local people insist Arthur Conan Doyle once stayed there.

It doesn't seem to be haunted.

Stanner Rocks, three miles west of Kington

8 A Place to Die for

Merrily felt very small and exposed.
　She was wearing jeans and a green fleece with a torn pocket. She had a canvas shoulder bag with her cigarettes inside and her phone. Around her neck was a chain with a tiny gold cross on it that was hidden by the neck of her grey T-shirt.
　Disoriented in an old town like a pop-up book, coming at her from all angles in wedges of carrot-coloured antique brick and twisting timbers and thrusting gables ...

The Smile of a Ghost

This is a novel about ... well, ghosts, kind of, but mainly about obsession. It's now slightly notorious for (a couple of years before the tragic Bridgend epidemic of 2008) having a theme of localised teenage suicide, linked, in this case, to a famous fall from the Hanging Tower of Ludlow Castle in south Shropshire.

Ludlow is a town which usually attracts less fatal obsession, but obsession nonetheless. People visit it and just have to live there – not only, perhaps, because of the recent boom in fancy restaurants, or even the fact that Ludlow is frequently named as the most beautiful medieval town in Britain. It could be something far more elusive, because it goes back centuries. Even 300 years ago, the town had a reputation as a resort ... somewhere it was good just to be.

In the novel, the notoriously gothic singer, Bell Pepper, known as Belladonna, moves to Ludlow and, for reasons which, if you haven't read the novel, you wouldn't want me to explain here, begins to roam its streets and passageways at night with a candle-lamp, like a ghost.

However, the novel's, and the town's, real ghost may be someone else.

Marion de la Bruyere

> There are two ways out of that tower, and I took the wrong one at first and came up against some steps that led nowhere any more, a blank wall, and that was horrifying, as if whichever way I went I'd come up against a wall that hadn't been there when I went in. Imagination, in these situations, becomes so unbelievably powerful. So I scrambled back down and back into the chamber and ... well ... that's when I saw her.
>
> Bernie Dunmore, Bishop of Hereford, *The Smile of a Ghost*

'A lady of the castle' is how Marion is usually described, which, when you think about it, could mean anything. She was probably very young when she died.

This was in the twelfth century, the reign of Henry II, whose predecessor, Stephen, had given control of Ludlow Castle to a Breton knight, Joce de Dinan, who may have left his name to Dinham, the sloping community between the castle and the River Teme.

Ludlow Castle is probably the most impressive medieval stronghold along the Welsh border. It has many royal connections, and was once the military HQ for Wales. In a honeyed light, it looks deceptively mellow. Except, possibly, for the Hanging Tower.

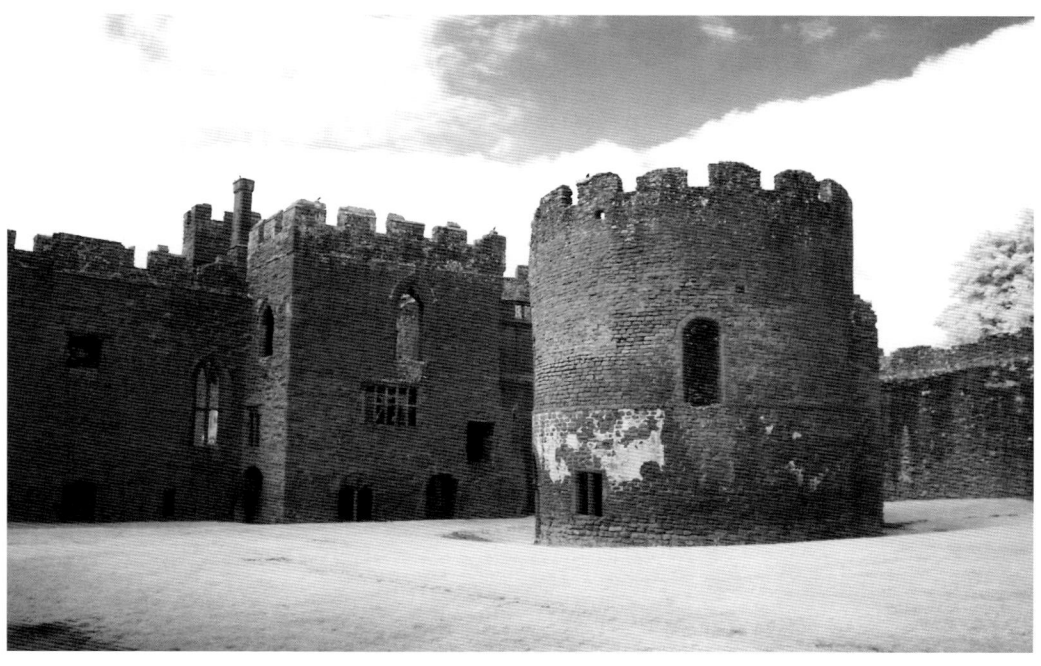

Ludlow Castle: the Round Chapel with part of the northern range behind

The baronial de Lacy family, big in the area, had coveted this castle for some time, and the Lacy/Dinan conflict had led to the capture of a young knight, Arnold de Lisle. While imprisoned in the castle, Arnold formed a relationship with Marion de la Bruyere, who helped him escape down a rope or possibly knotted sheets. Unfortunately she then let him back up by rope ladder and, during their rapturous reunion, a whole bunch of heavily-armed de Lacy men shot up the ladder and took the castle. Soon afterwards, there was much slaughter and destruction in the town to make it clear that de Lacy was now in control.

When she saw what she'd done, the remorseful Marion killed Arnold with his own sword and then, fearing either repercussions from Joce or gang-rape by de Lacy's heavies, threw herself from the highest window in the Hanging Tower. It was said that her final anguished screams could be heard for years afterwards before they were reduced to a breathing sound. In *A Gazetteer of British Ghosts*, Peter Underwood recalled a Ludlow man, Mr J. Didlick, 'who told me that the sounds might be likened to those made by someone in very deep sleep'.

Ludlow Castle: the view west from the tower of St Laurence's Church

So maybe she's at peace now.

I couldn't find Mr Didlick, but the Hanging Tower may be viewed from inside the castle, now owned by the Earl of Powis, whose home castle at Welshpool is in far better repair.

But, for a more dramatic – and cheaper – view of the tower, follow the public footpath to the right of the castle, as you approach it from the town centre. You'll eventually arrive at the yew tree under Marion's window, the subject of the chapter entitled Tonguing the Yew, in *The Smile of a Ghost*.

(Health and Safety warning: don't tongue the yew. Yews are very poisonous.)

Anyway, this is a significant point on Bell Pepper's ghost-walk, which you might prefer to start from the other end of town, beginning in —

St Leonard's Graveyard

Possibly my all-time favourite cemetery can be reached from the bottom of Corve Street by following the path alongside the former church, which now serves as a printing and copying workshop. The disused graveyard itself – and it's fair to say not everybody thinks this is a good thing – has been allowed to become atmospherically overgrown as a wildlife haven. It will lead you to some nicely-framed and unexpectedly green views of the castle across the town.

Ludlow: St Leonard's graveyard

Ludlow: The Feathers Hotel and a detail of the carving

Ludlow: The Butter Market, St Laurence's Church and Bodenham's

In fact, it's possible to walk from here to the castle avoiding all prominent streets and rarely encountering, even in high season, too many people ... although ghosts can't be ruled out as you wander through the yards of one-time coaching inns, up and down stone steps, along narrow alleyways, catching ribbons of conversation through open back doors as whole centuries seem to drop away.

You need to stop in the Linney, the steep, narrow street backing on to the castle's curtain wall before curving down to the River Teme. All very clean and refined now but it's easy to imagine medieval human detritus in full foetid flow down the earthen gutters to the river.

You will, by now, have passed through the shadow of the church sometimes called the Beacon of the Marches.

The Church of St Laurence

I once stayed in the centre of Ludlow for two months, while starting a new job, and the church clock awoke me every hour on the hour all through the night. It's been quietened now, which is a shame in a way. But the church is still as big a presence in the old town as the castle, and its foundations may be even older, built, as they were, out of a Neolithic mound, presumably the low in Ludlow.

St Laurence's, as you can see from the amazing vantage point at Whitcliffe – don't miss this view – is the centre of the wheel of Ludlow. If you have the stamina and a head for heights, you can climb to the top of the tower, scene of the climax of *Smile*, and take in dizzying views of the castle, the town and Clee Hill beyond. The vertiginous should at least check out the Palmers' Window inside the church, which commemorates —

Church of St Laurence, Ludlow: detail of vaulted ceiling and reredos

Church of St Laurence, Ludlow: misericords in the choir

The Palmers' Guild

A Palmer was a medieval pilgrim to the Holy Land who brought back a palm frond as evidence of having done the trip. The Palmers' Guild was mystically linked to the cult of King Edward the Confessor and to St John. You can get an idea of all this possibly-wishful thinking in the impressive fifteenth-century eight-paned Palmers' stained-glass window. More than just a collection of 'what we did on our pilgrimage' snaps.

The Guild, consisting mainly of wealthy businessmen, was formed to employ priests whose main function was to pray for the souls of Guild members and their families. In those days, buying a stairway to heaven was as legitimate as taking out a pension fund and, indeed, the Guild also fulfilled a similar role in supporting members who fell on hard times.

It's difficult, without one of those *look away now* moments, to explain the significance, in this novel, of the Palmers' Guild. But it's worth noting that, while there were similar guilds all over Britain, Ludlow's achieved national prominence.

Overleaf: Church of St Laurence, Ludlow: stained glass in the Palmers' Guild Chapel

9   Music of the Spheres

'Drivers reckoned they swerved to avoid a ghost,' Spicer said.
   His tone hadn't altered and his eyes remained limpid. A wood pigeon's hollow call was funnelled out of the valley.
   'That took a while to come, didn't it?' Merrily said.
                                    The Remains of an Altar

A<small>LTAR BEGINS</small> – and perhaps ends – with a ghost story, and the idea for the novel began with a real one.

A few years ago, villagers at Stoke Lacy, in eastern Herefordshire, came to believe that the road through their community was haunted, following a series of unexplained road accidents.

Most accidents involve more than one vehicle, maybe one driver swerving to avoid another. In Stoke Lacy, vehicles were leaving the road in isolation, drivers

British Camp and Midsummer Hill from the west

View north from British Camp along the Malvern Hills

saying it felt as if someone else was moving the steering wheel. It happened so many times that an exorcism was suggested, and there was consultation with the man who was standing in, at the time, for Merrily Watkins.

However, the deliverance minister for Hereford had a problem with it. For a start, there was no back-story – no famous death-crash in the past, no suggestion of an unquiet spirit which might benefit from a Requiem Eucharist, or even an imprint or place-memory. In the end he was unconvinced and took no action.

The only solution was offered by members of the British Society of Dowsers, who surveyed the road with rods and pendulums, and concluded that the problem had been caused by the siting of a millennial stone in a wood which they suggested may have been disrupting the energy flow, causing a reflex reaction in the motorists.

Either way, it made me think about unexplained road accidents, and that's how *The Remains of an Altar* begins – although not in Stoke Lacy – as Merrily Watkins is called in to investigate similar, if more extreme, accidents in the village of Wychehill.

View over the Severn Plain from the Malvern Hills, with Little Malvern Priory visible in the trees at the foot of the hills (bottom right).

To find the general area of this troubled community, take the main road northeast from Ledbury and turn left by the hotel near the British Camp car park. This puts you in the Malvern Hills ... which really are the remains of an altar.

We live just below the Black Mountains, and the Malverns are our easterly horizon. It's clear to anyone who lives or walks or drives around this area that there's a link between the Black Mountains of Wales and the Malverns (from the Welsh *moel bryn* – bald hill) of England. Two great, sacred shelves of rock enclosing Herefordshire's landscaped garden of lush pastures, orchards and hop-yards.

The English Heritage publication *The Malvern Hills, an Ancient Landscape*, by Mark Bowden, with David Field and Helen Winton, confirmed what I'd always felt: these hills, with the lofty earthworks of Herefordshire Beacon and Midsummer Hill, were the remains of an altar. Sacred. Untouchable. Full of earth energy and the life-force of water.

The Victorian spa of Great Malvern tapped into the healing power of mineral waters, but there was something here that was clearly recognised in Celtic and pre-Celtic times, when the earthworks were taking shape.

And later, in between the Celtic and Victorian eras, 'it is tempting,' say the authors of *An Ancient Landscape*, 'to consider the Malvern Hills as a "ritual landscape" in the medieval period as much as in the prehistoric periods'. The book goes on to identify the hills as a magnet for early Christian hermits, spiritually

Little Malvern Priory with the Malverns behind

challenged by the desolation and that sense of exposure, not only to the elements but to 'ancient practices and spirits'.

Out of Celtic Christian hermitages came the spiritual strongholds of Great Malvern and Little Malvern priories: '... the priories are not ordinary parish churches but rather the bases of religious "elite forces".'

Which somehow confirmed my idea of having an ex-SAS man as the vicar of Wychehill, letting me into some of the legends of The Regiment, based in Hereford.

But it was never going to be easy, or even possible, to write a novel set in the Malvern Hills without involving another legend – Britain's most famous composer.

I didn't know all that much about Sir Edward Elgar beyond the usual clichés: Master of the King's Music, 'Pomp and Circumstance', making Britain mightier yet ... This stiff, slightly aloof establishment figure wheeled out annually for The Last Night of the Proms.

However, after a few months' serious research, I was looking at a very different person: Ed, the Worcester piano-tuner's son who married above his class. Ed, the paranoid perfectionist, insecure, depressive, often in despair over his work. A man who actually loved *the country* more than The Country. Who wrote brilliant music but is too often associated with words he *didn't* write.

Whose high-Catholicism was sometimes challenged by an instinctive paganism. Whose friend and confidante, for some years, seems to have been his daughter's white rabbit, Peter.

And then there was another friend —

ED AND ALF

For some years, Edward Elgar, the composer, and Alfred Watkins, who discovered leys, were neighbours in Hereford.

This isn't widely known. But then, why would it be? While Hereford's connection with Elgar is always being underlined in the city and the pages of the *Hereford Times*, Watkins, who was born here and served Hereford all his working life, still gets more recognition outside. Far more.

It's bloody criminal, really. Sorry ... I keep going on about this. There should be an Alfred Watkins Museum and visitor centre in Hereford, but I expect the Establishment is worried about attracting undesirables with walking boots and dowsing rods.

Anyway, Elgar's famous residence, Plas Gwyn, now flats, is on the corner of the road which led to Watkins' house, The Vineyard (*see page 25*), where he lived before moving into the centre of the city.

Ed and Alfred were born within a year of one another. Both were into photography and gadgets. Elgar had a dark-room at Plas Gwyn and would have been fascinated by Watkins' various photographic inventions, including the first light-meter.

Edward Elgar, and Elgar's house, Plas Gwyn in Hereford

And then there was the countryside. Both men were members of the Woolhope Naturalists' Field Club. Both were drawn to a pastoral, very British kind of mysticism.

Why is this connection never referred to in major biographies of either of them? I don't know, but it seemed like an interesting thread for the novel.

I was haunted particularly by Elgar's *Cello Concerto* which, although it was written after he'd moved away from Malvern, seems to reflect the evening light and shadows on the hills and the *movement* of the hills. It was the *Cello Concerto*, on an early gramophone record, that drifted around the room where Elgar lay dying and which he whistled to a friend before he said,

> If ever you're walking on the Malvern Hills and hear that, don't be frightened ... it's only me.

And it *is* him. He haunts those hills. Especially Herefordshire Beacon with the earthworks on top like a dented sandwich cake.

Elgar's choral epic, *Caractacus*, recalls the legend (long ago discredited) that this was the site of the Ancient British hero's last stand against the Romans. The music is full of numinous shapes in the woods and druidic blood-ritual ... and it goes way over the top, thanks to the librettist's determination to turn it into a hymn to a British Empire far wider than Rome's puny effort.

'I did suggest we should dabble in patriotism in the Finale,' Elgar wrote later, 'when, lo!, the worder, instead of merely paddling his feet goes & gets naked & wallows in it ...'

British Camp, with its Norman motte visible on the skyline

All Elgar wallowed in was the mystery and the energy of the countryside, as he pedalled along the lanes around his home at Birchwood on his beloved bike Mr Phoebus – commemorated in the bronze sculpture on the cathedral green in Hereford – not far, as it happens, from Alfred Watkins' last home. Ed is leaning on Mr Phoebus peering up at the Cathedral, with big trees on either side, and on the plinth it says,

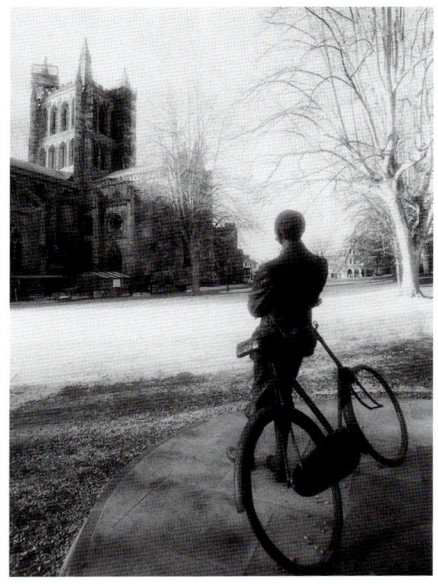

Elgar statue, Cathedral Close, Hereford

> This is what I get every day. The
> trees are singing my music –
> or am I singing theirs?

Elgar loved trees, was moved and inspired by them. While living in the south of England he once took his friend and musical collaborator Algernon Blackwood, ritual magician and author of classic ghost stories, including *The Man Whom the Trees Loved*, to see some oaks near his home which were said to be monks bewitched. He loved that story.

So it seemed inconceivable that Elgar, with that passion for trees and the interest in druidic ritual displayed in *Caractacus*, was not intimately familiar with the —

WHITELEAFED OAK

You'll find the oak – well, several of them – at the end of the Malvern Hills, almost exactly at the meeting point of the counties of Herefordshire, Worcestershire and Gloucestershire, the three counties that come together for the annual Three Choirs Festival, for which Elgar composed some of his finest sacred music.

This is also the centre of the circle of Perpetual Choirs, which I first read about in the works of John Michell, the writer who rediscovered Alfred Watkins in the 1960s and raised him to a new level of international fame in books including *The View over Atlantis*.

Essentially, Michell developed what Watkins himself had only hinted at – the idea that alignments of old stones and mounds and other landscape patterns were the remains of an ancient knowledge far more advanced than history recognises … reflecting a universal harmony most of us can no longer perceive.

The novel forms a curious link between all this and Elgar's most complex and profound choral work, *The Dream of Gerontius*, from Cardinal Newman's account of what happens to a man's soul after death ... a journey into the formal Roman Catholic afterlife with all its angelic bureaucracy. Not exactly easy-listening, often emotional and strangely tense.

And there's a moment that shoots right up your spine. A dangerous moment which the composer, conscious of sacrilege, nearly bottled, and ... this is where you need to read the novel, but it builds into an exploration of the ancient science of Pythagoras and the seductive theories of cosmic harmony and the Music of the Spheres.

And suppose Elgar *had* spent time at Whiteleafed Oak while agonising – and he really *did* agonise – over *Gerontius*?

Whiteleafed Oak is a hamlet, up a narrow lane from Hollybush, not far from Eastnor Castle. In a glass case on the village green you may find a curious little diagram related to *Harmonic Convergences* (or something). All a bit New Agey, but the significance gradually becomes apparent to Merrily Watkins in the course of *The Remains of an Altar*, as she and Lol Robinson learn about the Perpetual Choirs and meet the eccentric composer Tim Loste.

You can only reach the actual oaks on foot. It's about half a mile from the houses, across the fields. The original great oak, said to be a centre of Druid worship, at the end of a processional trail, is long gone, but its successor has been chosen. Amongst its boughs, in the wrinkles of its vast bole, you'll find offerings – ribbons and shiny things – left by recent pilgrims.

Now observe the newly-exposed views to the landmarks of the three counties.

And listen ...

Whiteleafed oak

10 Ghosts and Templars

Outside, a wind had arisen, chattering amongst dead chrysanths in a grave pot. Merrily pulled the church keys from her shoulder bag. The Master House key poked out and she thrust it back ...

The Fabric of Sin

RESEARCH FOR *The Fabric of Sin* uncovered the fact that not only had the Knights Templar church at Garway been visited by the – almost certainly – greatest-ever writer of ghost stories, M.R. James, but that *something happened to him there.*

Something disturbing, referred to obliquely but tantalisingly in a letter to his Herefordshire friend, Gwen MacBride.

It was a gift.

Everything in Garway seemed like a gift. Its history, its folklore, its very strange church, its dovecote with 666 dove-holes ... even the names of its pubs argued that something curious was, and may still be, at work in this landscape, a kind of inland peninsula of England dropping down to the River Monnow, on the other side of which is Wales.

It's not easy setting a novel in a very small community which actually exists. While I've always identified

M.R. James

real towns and a few larger villages, I get cold feet about inflicting murder, feuds and iffy history on a tiny community where people and houses could easily be (wrongly) identified.

Garway, though ... with Garway, there was no way around it. And it helped that the suggestion for a Garway novel came from a very long-established and respected local family, and all the people I spoke to were well aware of what I was doing and were *still* helpful. It was necessary to create the Master House, incorporating elements of other dwellings and acting as a catalyst for the floating weirdness, but most of the rest you can visit.

But let's approach this place, initially, in the company of the writer and academic, Montague Rhodes James.

M.R. JAMES (1862–1936)

This man is an example, still, for everybody who aspires to write a ghost story.

Although, of course, M.R. James didn't actually do ghosts. He mainly did ... things. Entities. Malevolent, terrifying entities. Think of what was inside the ash tree in the story of that name. The 'lungless laugh' from *A Warning to the Curious*. And, most important in the *Fabric of Sin* context, the 'face of crumpled linen' from *Oh Whistle and I'll Come to you, My Lad*.

A serious scholar, like several of his protagonists, Monty James, son of a clergyman in Suffolk, became provost of Eton and King's College, Cambridge, studied old manuscripts, church architecture, stained glass ... tombs.

And spent a lot of time in Herefordshire where he stayed with the widow of his friend James McBryde, who illustrated his first volume of ghost stories and died far too young. From 1906, Gwendolen McBryde and her daughter, Jane, lived near Kilpeck. Gwen seems to have been devoted to Monty in a platonic sort of way. He'd spend relaxing holidays with the McBrydes and became guardian to Jane, who displayed graphic skills from an early age and was also very fond of things emerging from gaping tombs.

Monty was especially fond of the McBrydes' second home in Herefordshire, from which he attended services at Dore Abbey. In her book, *Letters to a Friend*, Gwendolen recalled him reading the lesson in 'his fine, slightly plaintive voice ... It always gave me an unreal feeling, as if some saint held forth to lesser creatures and birds.'

Although he said Hereford Cathedral may have been one of the locations behind *The Stalls of Barchester*, the only M.R. James story set wholly in Herefordshire was *A View from a Hill*, the one involving strange visions seen through a particular pair of binoculars.

Oh Whistle and I'll Come to you, My Lad involves the ruins of a Knights Templar preceptory. In the story, this is in Monty's native Suffolk, probably Felixstowe.

But some of the best preserved and most mysterious Templar remains in the country are to be found at Garway.

The Knights Templar

For more than seven centuries, this order of medieval warrior monks has been gathering mystique like fairy dust. Established in the twelfth century to protect Christian pilgrims, The Order of the Poor Knights of Christ and the Temple of Solomon got rich quick, having become the first international bankers and – allegedly – discovered lost treasures on the site of the famous temple in Jerusalem where they were based.

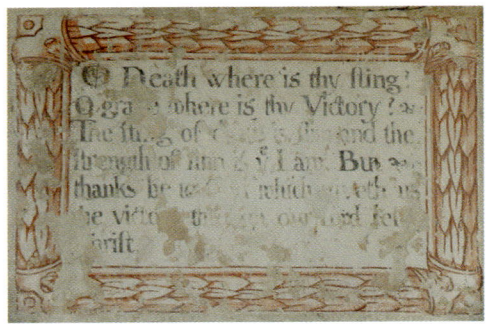

Dore Abbey and two of its wall paintings

Were they the guardians of the Holy Grail? And what was the Holy Grail? According to the cult 1980s best-seller, *The Holy Blood and the Holy Grail*, later fictionalised in *The Da Vinci Code*, the Grail legends obscure the bloodline of Jesus and Mary Magdalene, who apparently were an item.

Garway Church, with a detail of the Norman chancel arch (top)

Or not. In *The Fabric of Sin*, I left all this alone and concentrated on the Templars themselves and, particularly, their last Grand Master, Jacques de Molay, who is said to have spent time in Garway.

You can read about all this in Audrey Tapper's *Knights Templar & Hospitaller in Herefordshire*, which collects all the known facts about Garway and the other local Templar sites, principally at Dinmore, so I'm not going to pinch Audrey's research here. Anyway, novels let you develop the facts.

The Church of St Michael (yes, another one)

Not much has actually changed in Garway since the Templar church was handed over to their successors, the Hospitallers. You can still see the remains of the circular nave, built in imitation of the Church of the Holy Sepulchre in Jerusalem. The sandstone tower, which seems to wear a kind of sardonic little smile and was originally separated from the body of the church, was also built by the Templars, whose stone coffin lids you'll find in window ledges and the chancel steps.

Templars everywhere. Still. And what exactly are those golden figures which appear in the picture I snapped when the red curtain was drawn across the nave (*see page 19*)?

Garway Church is small, unspoiled but *never* cosy. An experienced dowser, exploring the interior with Sir Richard Heygate during research for Richard's book, with Philip Carr-Gomm, *English Magic*, in 2008, said he'd experienced a shattering sense of evil in the area of the piscina, once used to wash the communion chalice.

Personally, I've never detected any evil here, but there's certainly a pervading air of secrecy. I was in the church one dappled autumn morning, with my wife, Carol, and local historian Sue Rice, when the dowser and Egyptologist John Ward perambulated the tower and suggested there was a secret room in which something had been kept. Outside, he arranged us all around a field where he'd dowsed the outline of a vanished building.

There's a lot still to be found here.

On the edge of farm buildings behind the church, the holy spring trickles, overhung by small, ribbony offerings – perhaps

Garway: the Holy Well

Garway: the Columbarium

the water supply which first commended this place as a religious settlement.

Follow the stream to the edge of the churchyard, and there, among the farm buildings you can see the Columbarium, like a kiln.

The dovecote. Probably built by the Templars and improved by the Hospitallers. One of the finest, best-preserved medieval dovecotes in Britain, its dove-chambers numbering an enigmatic 666. The Number of the Beast ... possibly. Nobody knows why it has this exact number of chambers, but the stone plinth in the middle is unlikely to be an altar to Satan.

This is where Merrily and Jane have that first fateful meeting with Mrs Morningwood, the alternative therapist and possibly one of the Nine Witches of Garway (we'll get to them).

Meanwhile, back in the church, on the left side of the chancel arch, you need to meet someone else.

The Green Man

Examples of the Green Man are found in churches all over Britain, with several in Herefordshire. A male face peers through twigs and leaves, teeth clenched around them. The foliate face is normally considered a pagan fertility symbol, but nobody

Garway Church: the Green Man

really knows and nobody knows, either, why it's found in Christian churches.

Garway's Green Man however, is subtly different. As Sue Rice has pointed out, whatever is issuing from his mouth seems more like a cord with tassels than foliage ... and the cord is associated with Baphomet, the bearded head which the Knights Templar were said to have venerated and which was later turned into a scarily androgynous symbol sometimes connected with black magic.

The image of the Green Man filters through history and has royal connections. Charles II, peering through the branches of an oak tree while hiding from his enemies, is one example. The latest one, of course, is the Prince of Wales, champion of organic farming, energy conservation and alternative therapies, who may, apparently – given the problems encountered by the two previous King Charleses – decide to adopt another name on accession to the throne.

The Prince's business, The Duchy of Cornwall owns many thousands of acres in Herefordshire and acquired the Harewood Estate, only a few miles from Garway, where a working hamlet is being rebuilt, along with a large house.

The Harewood Estate also has a Knights Templar chapel.

It seemed reasonable that the Duchy, which owns many farms, should buy the Master House, so called because of its connection with Jacques de Molay, last Grand Master of the order.

De Molay was publicly burned in Paris after charges of heresy and borderline satanic worship were laid against the Templars by the King of France, Philip the Fair, and his friend the Pope. The basis of these charges seems to lie in the fact that the Templars were very rich and the King of France needed the money, but Baphomet doesn't seem to have been an invention of the prosecution and it's arguable that some Templar communities had become corrupted. My feeling is that de Molay himself, while a bit of an operator, was probably on the side of the angels. The climax of *The Fabric of Sin*, in which Jacques is remembered, occurs on the seven-hundredth anniversary of his death.

Jacques de Molay

But let's return to M.R. James who, during a holiday in Herefordshire, went one day, with either Jane or Gwendolen or both of them, to visit Garway Church. A memorable visit, which he referred to later in a letter to Gwendolen:

> We must have offended somebody or something at Garway, I think. Probably we took it too much for granted, in speaking of it, that we should be able to do exactly as we pleased. Next time we shall know better. There is no doubt that it is a very rum place and needs careful handling.

Now, it could be that they simply left a gate open and were pursued by a farmer with a stick. And yet it's very much the sort of thing people say in an M.R. James ghost story. 'Somebody or something.' And it's the place that he describes as rum and in need of careful handling.

This figures.

M.R. James was often asked if he actually believed in ghosts and his careful reply was that he was prepared to consider the evidence.

In putting *Fabric* together, I looked at the plot of *Oh Whistle* ... which does involve an actual whistle, found by a visiting academic in the remains of those Knights Templar ruins in Suffolk. When he blows it he summons the wind ... and something else. Something made out of rumpled bedclothes, with a face of crumpled linen.

The sign for The Garway Moon

As recorded by Ella Mary Leather, 'whistling up the wind' was once common practice amongst Herefordshire farmers, to bring on a winnowing breeze. From Mrs Leather, too, I learned that Garway was one of the last places to maintain the *watch after death*, in which the whole household sat up all night when someone died on the premises. A pewter plate of salt was placed on the body, with a candle in its centre. I started to interweave these stories to seek out an explanation of Monty's reference to a *rum place*.

And it *is* a rum place. It did have four pubs, all linked to the heavens – the Sun, the Moon (the only one still open), the Globe and the Seven Stars.

And it did have that old saying,

> There'll be nine witches from the bottom of Orcop to the end of Garway Hill as long as water flows …

Candidates for the Nine are identified to this day.

Overleaf: a sign for The Sun, Garway (not an inn but a one-time shop that went by the same name)

11 The Uncoiling of the Serpent

The landscape itself was throwing off centuries like superfluous bedclothes, an old light pulsing to the surface, and Jane could feel the urgency of it in her spine.

To Dream of the Dead

Archaeologists are feeling this, too, in the wake of the finding of The Dinedor Serpent, or The Rotherwas Ribbon as it was originally and more prosaically called by local councillors who were wishing it would just curl up and die.

The subplot of *The Remains of an Altar* involved the discovery of ancient stones under a site in Coleman's Meadow, Ledwardine which Herefordshire Council had earmarked for development. In the book, this led to major protests, involving environmental, heritage and pagan factions, led, of course, by Jane Watkins.

Even as that book was being prepared for publication, archaeologists were uncovering what was described as a unique Bronze Age ritual construction ... right in the path of a new road planned by that same local authority.

It was almost uncanny, and there was no way I could get out of using the Dinedor Serpent in a future novel. Especially as it, too, generated a massive row, with the council accused of – literally – a cover-up in its determination to make sure the road went through.

A man chained himself to a JCB and eight people were arrested for aggravated trespass for refusing to leave the council's HQ, where the issue was to be

Rotherwas Chapel: exterior and chancel

discussed in private. Because there weren't enough spare cells at Hereford, some of them were taken to Worcester, where they languished for hours. 'I spent the time psychically cleansing my cell,' one woman said.

In the end, all charges were dropped, but it left a nasty taste.

Rotherwas has not, in recent years, been the most favoured part of Hereford. Industrial estates – and Rotherwas has Hereford's biggest – are seldom scenic. The area's architectural jewel, Rotherwas Chapel, Elizabethan family chapel of the Catholic Bodenhams, is just round the corner from the public dump.

But the chapel, the dump and the factories all share the city's finest backdrop: Dinedor Hill, with its woodland and its Celtic camp.

And now the Dinedor Serpent, which the Council has always preferred to refer to as the Rotherwas Ribbon – far less sexy; who would ever want to visit that?

THE SERPENT

So ... what exactly is it, and why was it constructed?

Well, of course, we don't know.

It was found during a routine archaeological scan of the proposed site of the Rotherwas relief road – a planned shortcut out of the industrial estate.

There never was, to be honest, much to see.

In *To Dream of the Dead*, a councillor dismisses the Serpent as 'patio gravel'.

Me (on right) standing alongside dowser Chris Hinsley and The Serpent 'path'

Which, as you can see in the picture above (part of the Serpent is exposed behind me and the dowser Chris Hinsley – he's the one with the beard) is not entirely insulting.

The small stones are believed to be fire-cracked, the result of rocks dropped into a burning pit. The original theory was that they were then used for the surface of a path, some kind of ritual walkway possibly all the way from the top of Dinedor Hill to the River Wye. But the fact that there was no substructure suggested they weren't exactly for walking on.

Could they simply have been chippings thrown away after the stones had been used for some other purpose – the first industrial waste to be dumped at Rotherwas? But why were so many of the fragments found to be quartz?

Archaeologists began to consider the idea that because of the quartz content, likely to glow in the moonlight, the curving path could have been intended as some kind of Bronze Age special-effect, reflecting the meandering of the river. Awesome under a full moon.

Somehow, it answers all the criteria for an authentic spirit path, connecting the sacred river (rivers were seen as entrances to the otherworld) with Hereford's holy hill. Unsuitable for human beings, a point of access for the ancestors.

If it is a monument, the only comparable ones are the Serpent Mounds of Ohio, conserved at huge expense. As an American said, on hearing about Dinedor, 'We'd kill to have a find like that.'

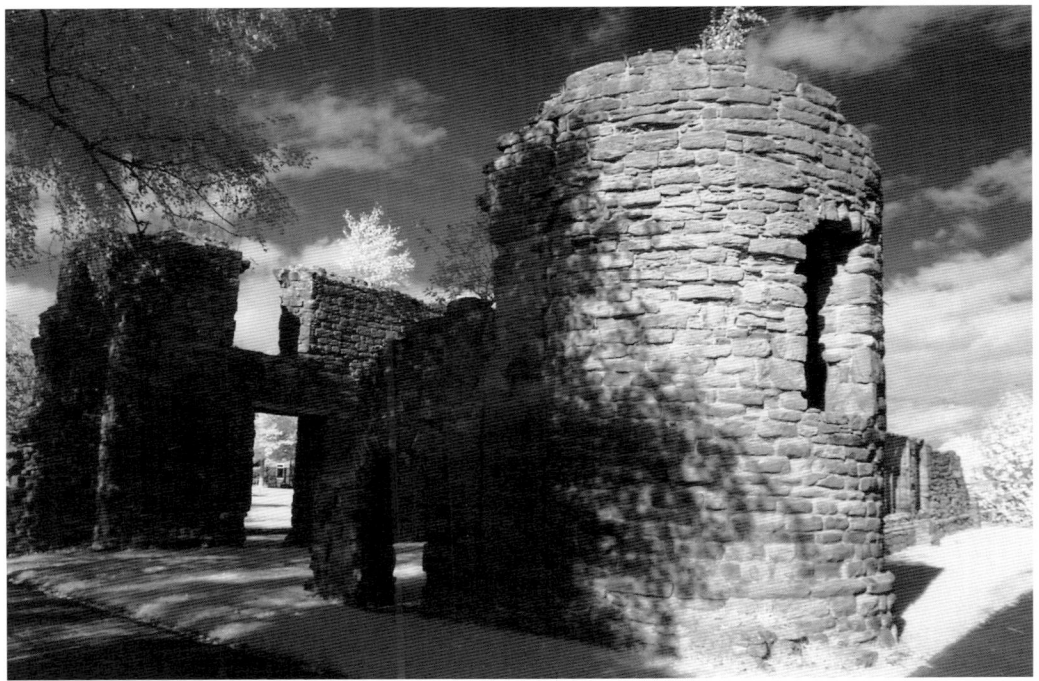

Above and opposite: Blackfriars Monastery, Hereford

In *To Dream of the Dead*, someone *is* killed, part of him displayed on the preaching cross near to the ruins of the Blackfriars Monastery, which crouch behind the medieval Coningsby Hospital in Widemarsh Street.

In some cities the Blackfriars Monastery would be a major tourist attraction. In Hereford it's a secret. Wander in there, the chances are you'll be on your own. But at least it's conserved.

The future of the Serpent remains unclear. The road is now open. Archaeologists tended to agree that the only way of preserving the remains was to cover them up, but the bitter irony of having industrial traffic roaring over a possible ritual path has not gone unnoticed.

The new Rotherwas road

The day before *To Dream of the Dead* was published, the *Hereford Journal* published a reader's letter as a page lead under the headline:

**Look out for the curse
of the Dinedor Serpent**

The letter more or less suggested that Hereford Council, by going ahead with the road out of Rotherwas, had opened up its own fast-track to hell ...

For many local people, the idea of hell is what the Council might have in mind for the green countryside now opened up by the road.

In *To Dream*, the parallels between the Serpent and the Coleman's Meadow excavation are underlined again.

Climate change is coming to Ledwardine, as it has to many local villages which had never been flooded until the new millennium. Jane Watkins, mindful of Nick Drake's somehow sinister song 'River Man', attempts to communicate with the worryingly swelling river which, for as long as anyone can remember, has been seeping sluggishly under the bridge at Ledwardine but is now getting greedy.

Meanwhile, a corporate chill hangs over the city of Hereford, where the felling of town-centre trees and the closure of local businesses, including the city's best and friendliest department store, Chadd's, signals a slippage into what Frannie Bliss, of Hereford CID, calls Landfill Britain.

To Dream of the Dead reflects the spread of a new unease in modern Hereford as its distant past is revealed.

Arthur's Stone

Further investigations in Rotherwas have uncovered indications of more extensive prehistoric settlement. Meanwhile, the county's first henge has been discovered in the Lugg Valley.

Ancient Hereford-shire has been neglected. The current thinking is that this area was far more important in the Neolithic world than was previously assumed. At present, its most prominent prehistoric monuments are Arthur's Stone, a burial chamber near Dorstone visited by Jane and her boyfriend Eirion in *The Remains of an Altar*, the Queen Stone in the Wye Valley and the Wern Derys standing stone, near Michaelchurch Escley, pictured on the cover of *To Dream of the Dead*.

The title of which comes from an old saying noted by Ella Mary Leather in *The Folk-lore of Herefordshire*:

> To Dream of the Dead is a sign of rain.

How would anyone come up with a saying like that?
Only on the Border ...

Overleaf: the Wern Derys standing stone

12 Gods of War

A treasure house. Out here in the deep sticks it was all so entirely unexpected as to be approaching the surreal.

The Secrets of Pain

Stories in the Merrily Watkins series usually start with the location. Initially, this one seemed unpromising.

At the core of *The Secrets of Pain* is the SAS, so that meant the flat countryside around Credenhill, an untidy village getting slowly sucked into Hereford City, as new roads and the new livestock market open up development potential. An area which tourists cruise past in search of the more obviously scenic and historic.

But those flat, empty fields alongside the A438 – the Brecon Road – host the ghosts that William Wordsworth saw.

> *While poring Antiquarians search the ground*
> *Upturned with curious pains, the Bard, a Seer,*
> *Takes fire: – The men that have been reappear;*
> *Romans for travel girt, for business gowned;*
> *And some recline on couches, myrtle gowned,*
> *In festal glee: why not?*

This lesser-known poem is entitled simply:

ROMAN ANTIQUITIES DISCOVERED AT BISHOPSTONE, HEREFORDSHIRE

The windows to William (left) and Dorothy Wordsworth (above) in Brinsop Church. Below: a view up the Wye at Weir Gardens, the site of a Roman villa

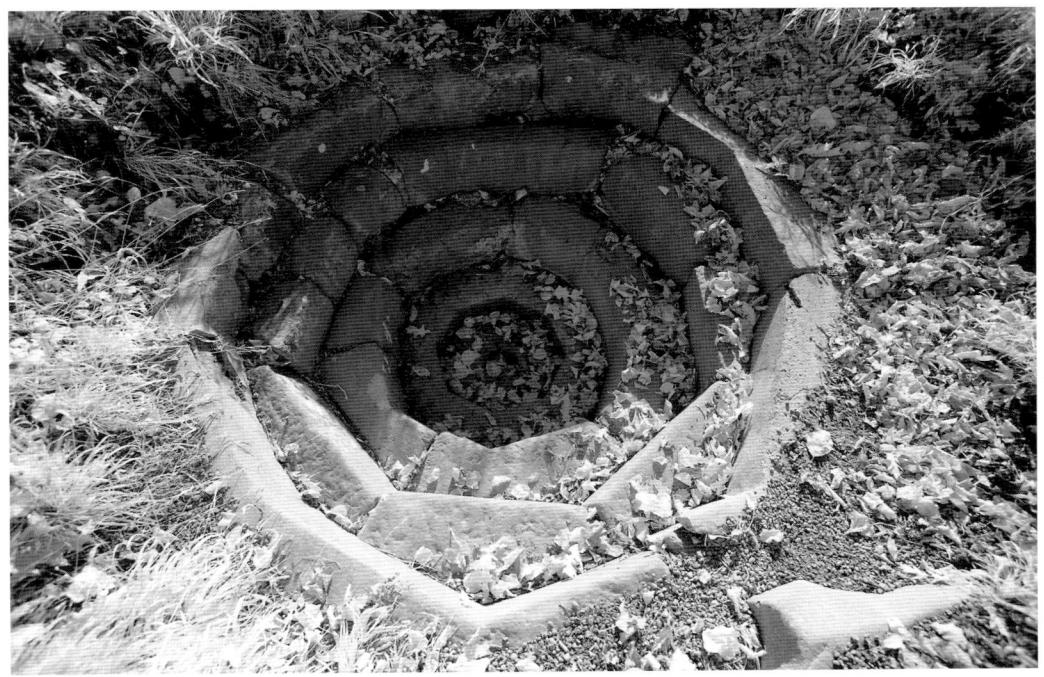

The possible Roman shrine near the entrance to the gardens at the Weir

— and was written while the poet was staying with his wife's cousin, Thomas Hutchinson, who was leasing the fourteenth-century Brinsop Court, a mile or so outside Credenhill. Wordsworth first visited the Court in 1827 and planted a tree that still stands outside the house. Brinsop Church (about which more later) has a stained glass window in his memory.

Not many people know this. I didn't. Nor did I know much about the Romans in Herefordshire, because there really isn't much to see. The little shrine near the entrance to the National Trust Weir Gardens, a handful of miles to the west, is not much more than a hole in the ground. Although the gardens offer some of the most interesting views of the River Wye west of Symonds Yat, the best of Roman Hereford is long gone.

Magnis, later known as Kenchester, was a substantial Roman town built close to the sacred River Wye on the route from Caerleon to Chester. In the first century AD, it had streets of shops and industrial buildings and suburban homes. Most of the stonework was plundered over the centuries for church buildings and the foundations of the new city growing a few miles away. 'Of the decay of Kenchester,' wrote John Leland, the Tudor antiquarian, 'Hereford rose and flourished.' But there was still plenty to see when William Stukeley checked it out towards the end of the eighteenth century:

GODS OF WAR

> A very fine mosaic floor a few years ago was found intire [sic], soon torn to pieces by the ignorant and vulgar. I took up some remaining stones of different colours, and several bits of fine potter's ware of red earth ... All around the city you may easily trace the walls, some stones being left everywhere, though overgrown by hedges and timber trees.

Interestingly, the most significant discoveries were made while *The Secrets of Pain* was being written, in 2010. The construction of the Yazor Brook Flood Alleviation Scheme meant that rescue-archaeologists were allowed into the Credenhill area ahead of the contractors. Significant Roman remains were soon unearthed, including the one that made the *Daily Mail*:

> **Archaeologists find 'muscular' body of British 'female gladiator'**
>
> Archaeologists have uncovered the remains of a 'massive, muscular woman' who may have been a female gladiator during the Roman occupation of Britain.
>
> The woman was buried in an elaborate wooden coffin with iron straps and copper strips in Credenhill, Herefordshire – close to the headquarters of the SAS.
>
> Her remains were found in a crouched position in an area thought to be a suburb of the nearby Roman town of Kenchester.

Archaeologists swiftly denied that there was any evidence that the woman had been a star of the arena, although it did give me an idea for a modern character of similar build called Victoria Buckland. The Roman history used in *The Secrets of Pain* was, however, strongly male-oriented, because *Magnis* began as a military base. 'A landscape quietly dedicated to war', is how the area is described to Merrily Watkins and Lol Robinson.

And of course it still is. On the edge of vanished *Magnis*, in a fork made by two Roman roads, lies an unassuming assembly of huts, served by a network of new roads. A substantial military village, with high wire fences and armed guards, this former RAF base is now the headquarters of the Special Air Service.

The SAS, formed during the Second World War, was and is an elite fighting force, highly trained to operate secretly behind enemy lines. It's responsible for many of the modern Hereford legends. In *Who Dares Wins*, his official biography of The Regiment, Tony Geraghty quotes an SAS instructor:

Opposite: one of the paths around the Iron Age fort at Credenhill

> 'One moment the world is a nice place, calm and quiet and beautiful. The next moment it is bloody chaos and you are going to die unless you react with total outright violence.'

From this came the sound-bite from Syd Spicer which burns itself into Merrily's consciousness.

> '... when you know that a difficult situation can only be resolved by an act of swift, efficient, intense and quite colossal violence.'

Syd, who first appeared in *The Remains of an Altar*, is an ex-SAS man turned clergyman, as some do. No big surprise. Tony Geraghty remarks that the SAS has its own kind of mysticism.

He also notes that, 'for some it is the living on after the action that requires the final reserves of courage'.

Which led me, inevitably, to *Baptism of Fire*, the autobiography of Frank Collins, the SAS man who was there in the Regiment's most public moments – when live TV tracked the Operation Nimrod team's arrival on the roof of the Iranian embassy to liberate 19 hostages.

Frank Collins later became, like Syd Spicer, a clergyman – curate, for a time, at St Peter's, Hereford, before rejoining the Army as a chaplain. He was forced to resign after failing to obtain permission to publish *Baptism of Fire*, which reveals some of the more disturbing aspects of life in the Regiment. The SAS often creates stronger ties than a family, and the resulting depression probably led to his suicide in 1998.

A significant quote from Frank Collins' book found its way into *The Secrets of Pain*.

> 'They're all mad in one way or another. There's Kev, who knows he's a reincarnated Viking. There's Si, who only reads books about the paranormal ... Only a few of the boys are normal, but they're so normal they're weird. What a bunch of crazies we are. And we go out with our lethal weapons every day.'

Obviously, I've met a few SAS men, but I didn't consult any of them directly about the developments in *Secrets*. A source close to the Regiment said, 'They like all the novels and the sensationalism. It adds to the mystique, and the mystique is very important. All they don't like is leaks ...'.

I'm not aware of any SAS men following the particular channel of paganism explored in *Secrets*, but another highly-informed source said, 'Wouldn't surprise me at all.' So that was all right.

'It's been read ... at the Camp,' I was told quietly, a few weeks after the book came out.

The SAS, it seems, likes a landscape moulded for defence. The Regiment's first base was near Dinedor Hill on the edge of Hereford City. Today, Credenhill's wooded flank forms its eastern horizon – another fortified hill, once the biggest Iron Age camp in Herefordshire, now a country park, with scenic walks. Not far from its base is the hamlet of Brinsop, with its fourteenth-century Court and a fascinating little church, which proved to be not only another significant component of the *Secrets* story but probably the central one.

On the outside, it looks quite modest, on its own, next to a field of sheep and lambs. Plain and solid, like a mid-Wales church, no steeple, just a small bell-tower. One of its biggest gravestones is the memorial to William and Dorothy Wordsworth's employee, Jane Winder, who travelled with them and died at Brinsop.

But the elevated churchyard suggests that the medieval church replaced a more rudimentary pre-Christian place of worship. You can imagine a circle of stones here, overlooking the very old moat which you can still see between the churchyard and the forestry at the foot of Credenhill. The humps in the higher land behind the church suggest there was once a substantial village, but now the only other nearby structure is in the sheep field below.

This is the Dragon's Well.

A stile gives access to the squat stone and a drain cover concealing the well. This dragon is the monster serpent reportedly slain by the patron saint of England, St George, and this is where the confrontation is said to have occurred.

George and the Dragon are all over Brinsop. Inside the church, the early twentieth-century embellishments by Sir William Comber show the traditional George as a knight in armour, his lance, typically, down the dragon's throat.

But on an early-medieval Romanesque tympanum, now on a wall of the nave, he's seen as a Roman soldier – more fitting, because this church is on the edge of Roman Hereford, and the carvings on this stone suggest another explanation explored in the novel.

The Dragon's Well

Above: Images of St George at Brinsop Church, clockwise from top left, on a banner, in stained glass, on a Romanesque tympanum and as a statue. Opposite: The Church of St George, Brinsop

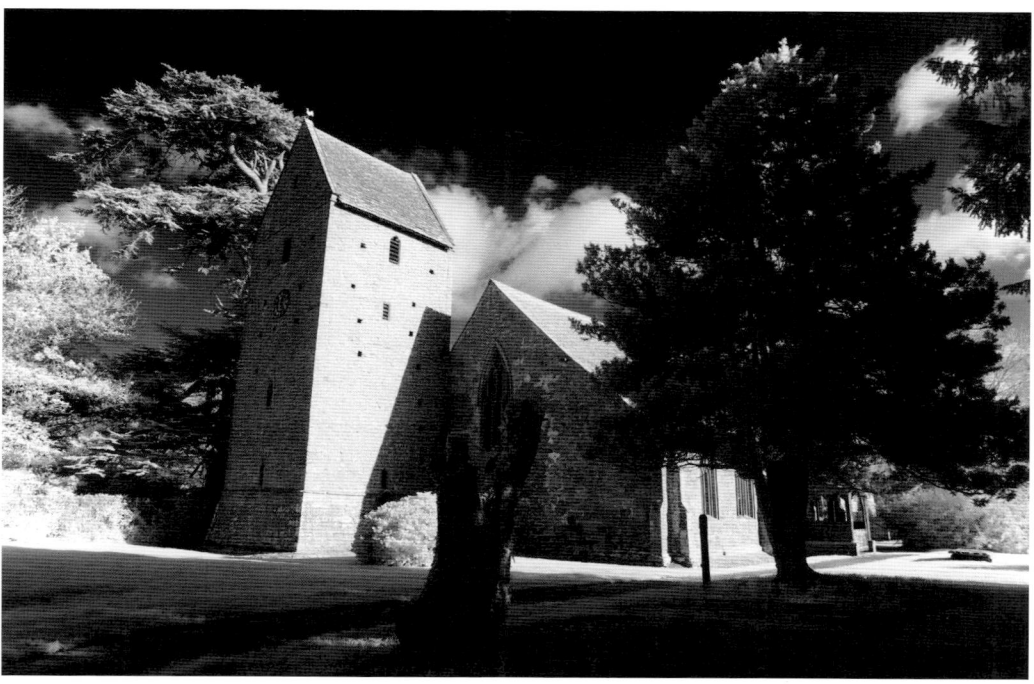

Top: Yazor Church. Below: Kinnersley Church

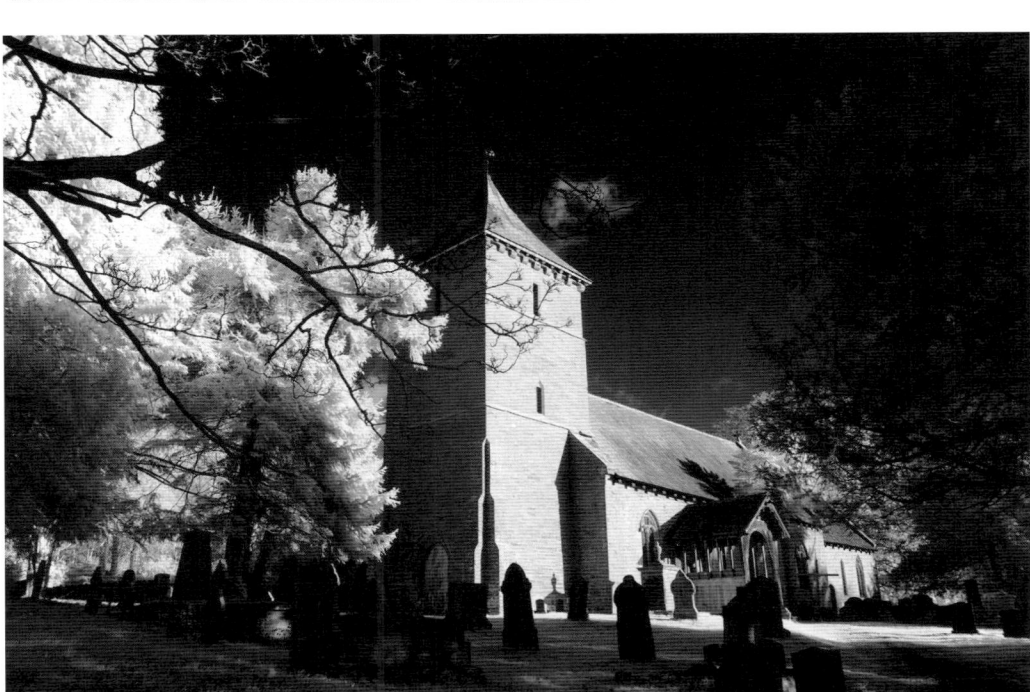

Top: Mansell Lacy Church. Below: Credenhill Church

East Street, Hereford. Alfred Watkins' last house lies behind the buildings on the left

On the wall beside the doorway you can see the mistily poignant remains of a mural: the Crucifixion, picking up on another theme from *Secrets*. It makes the Comber stuff look a little glitzy.

There's no monument here – or anywhere – to the great Alfred Watkins, unless you include the church itself and the other three of medieval (and probably earlier) origins – Mansell Lacy, Yazor and Kinnersley – which form a clear straight line through Brinsop to the mother hill behind.

In the City of Hereford, the last home of Alfred Watkins near the Cathedral is linked by a narrow alleyway to East Street, where, in *The Secrets of Pain*, a double murder is linked to the fruit farms whose polytunnels lie like worm casts in the fields around *Magnis*.

The Lol Robinson song, 'The Simple Trackway Man', on the CD, *A Message from the Morning*, is dedicated to AW.

> *I am a simple trackway man*
> *As walks the lanes by ancient plan*
> *Leading the people from beacon to steeple*
> *And steeple to stone*
> *And all the way home.*

13 The Keys to the Kingdom

It was nearing midnight, a waxing moon and stars on show – not much light-pollution from Hay, no traffic, no people. When Gwenda's bar had closed and his drinking companions had gone home, Robin had walked the empty sloping streets, up and down stone steps, across cobbles, for over an hour, intent on clearing his head. But his head had only filled up with the town. Starting with the gothic clocktower, starlit, moonlicked, a fairytale touch ...

The Magus of Hay

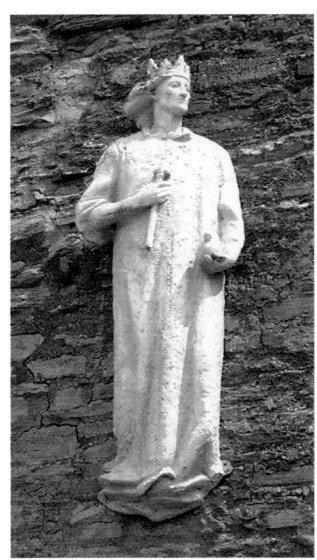

Sculpture to a king high on a wall by Hay's Market Square

Hay-on-Wye: you really couldn't make it up ... but let's try.

There's this small agricultural town on the edge of Mid-Wales, economically-challenged like most of them, which decides to start farming second-hand books.

Within a few years, it has around 40 bookshops.

And a King.

The King is Richard Booth, pioneer of the Hay book trade. He has a crown with jewels taken from a fancy dog-collar. He has a robe with fake ermine, and he carries an orb made from a lavatory ballcock.

People laugh at King Richard. But not for long.

Hay sits right on the Border, just inside Wales but with a Herefordshire postal address that fools Midland TV news editors into thinking it's in their patch.

Hay-on-Wye, town of books

Even before his coronation, Richard Booth had decided Hay should be independent of both Wales and England. The Wales Tourist Board and the Development Board for Rural Wales should be banned from the town, along with national supermarkets and chain stores. Local councils should, wherever possible, be ignored.

'Hay-on-Wye is the first town in the British Isles which has expressed its intention of declaring independence from the bureaucratic control of Central Government,' the King announced. He was wearing his robes and crown and puffing on a forearm-length Mexican cigar. His Cabinet, in jeans and scruffy sweaters, posed for the media, while a journalist asked the King if he was serious.

'Of course not,' he said. 'But it's more serious than real politics.'

And so it proved.

Soon, Hay was attracting book-tourists from all over the world, had become the most successful small town in the whole of Wales. The country's most famous inland resort.

And it was nothing to do with The Establishment.

The quangos (quasi-autonomous non-governmental organisations) had indeed somehow been shut out. There were no chainstores – even Boots the chemist soon

Hay Castle

disappeared, leaving Hay to Jones the local chemist's. The only supermarket – the Co-op – is, as it happens, just over the English border.

More booksellers moved in. Local people who might not otherwise have become booksellers found a new vocation. Individual supportive businesses – a greengrocer's, a rural delicatessen, a handful of new eateries – began to appear between the bookshops. Some also sold books – you can even find a few in the venerable jewellers', Mayalls – as if books have become a necessary talisman, a lucky charm.

Building on Hay's international reputation, a book festival, which began in a small way around the pubs in the town, became the biggest event of its kind in the country, bringing in tens of thousands of visitors and attracting the world's most famous writers, as well as leading politicians, musicians and movie stars. One year it included both Bill Clinton and Paul McCartney.

It was like a fairy tale, and in the tradition of fairy tales, the King bought Hay Castle and moved in thousands of second-hand books – books having already filled up the former fire station and the former cinema. A thriving economy had grown out of what can only be described as a modern myth. A legend. A piece

Hay Castle gateway and keep from the outside (top) and inside (bottom)

of contemporary folklore. It's difficult to think of anything similar happening anywhere else, ever.

It was as though Richard Booth's inspired move had attracted a strange kind of energy; as though some kind of independence had, on some level, actually occurred.

This little grey-brown town between the Black Mountains and the River Wye had acquired a strangely exotic ambience. Something slightly magical about it.

Which gave me the central idea for *The Magus of Hay*.

THE CASTLES

It's not easy setting a novel – particularly a thriller – in a real place, with a story that involves real, living people. You can't put words into the mouths of people who know that you know they didn't utter them.

But you can have your characters talking about real people, operating around them. And you can risk a possible small walk-on part for the King himself, just to show that, like the castle on the cover of *The Magus of Hay*, he actually exists.

Hay Castle is a mongrel, with a Norman gateway and the remains of a Jacobean mansion and some Victorian bits and … you get the idea. Windsor Castle just wouldn't work in Hay.

The Magus of Hay never goes inside the castle. There's no need to. But it's there as a living symbol of medieval Hay and a legacy of violence that not everyone in this novel wants to forget.

Your best source book for the early medieval history of Hay Castle is actually a novel, Barbara Erskine's *Lady of Hay*, published in 1986. This is the story of a woman hypnotically regressed into the persona of Mathilda – sometimes called Maud – who is said to have built the castle. Mathilda was married to William de Braose, the archetypal Norman baron who ran this part of the border in the days of King John. Like his king, de Braose, who has a historical role in *The Magus of Hay*, was not always portrayed as a bad guy, but mostly he was. What matters more in *Magus* is how he's perceived.

Back in the twentieth century, things didn't always go right for King Richard. The Booth business sometimes teetered on the brink of bankruptcy, and a good part of the castle was destroyed by fire, apparently started by a large rogue log in the hearth. But even that's a part of tradition on the Welsh border, where most castles have been torched and plundered at one time or another.

As this was the first novel explicitly about Hay since Barbara Erskine's book, which also involves the paranormal, I wanted a title that didn't sound like *Lady of Hay*. My first idea was *The Turning of Hay*, which I thought had a nice agricultural feel while also echoing Henry James' classic ghost story, *The Turn of the Screw*.

Unfortunately nobody at the publishing end liked it, and the only other title I came up with that they did like was *The Magus of Hay*.

Barbara says she doesn't mind.

The late, great Rob Soldat, historian and folklorist, and himself a medieval-looking figure on the streets of Hay, told me some stories about the castle, including one about a bloodstain that wouldn't go away – a story which, in the end, I didn't use because my novel never needed to go inside. What was important was that the castle was there, crowning the town, frowning over the market place.

The streets of old Hay curl up from the bank of the River Wye to the castle's curtain walls. If you look at a street plan, you can see they form the shape of a heart. I've examined it on several maps and Google Earth, and the heart is always apparent. The castle isn't part of it.

Closest to the castle is the alleyway known as Back Fold, home to Haydn Pugh's Juke Joint, next to which, in the novel, sit Jeeter Kapoor's cricket bookshop and Thorogoods' Pagan Books. But before the shops were here, Back Fold was the home of the castle's abattoir, and the tradition of slaughter continued until relatively recently.

Left: the narrow end of Back Fold. Right: Waterfall at Cusop

Interestingly, Hay once had two castles. Of the other, far smaller one, only the mound remains, down near the parish church. We don't really know when or why it was abandoned and why the big castle was built much further away from the river, which must have been far more important to Hay then than it is now.

The River

The Wye is surely the most revered river in southern Britain, but in Hay, you really have to search for it. Even the road bridge crossing the river from old Breconshire to old Radnorshire is the least-obvious road out of town. And in the town itself, I'm fairly sure, there are no signs pointing to the water's edge. Like Builth Wells, the next town upriver, Hay has turned its back on the Wye. To get a glimpse of it from the town, you need to climb up to the castle.

The best actual riverside walk leads from a footpath between the old castle mound and the parish church, past a waterfall and a scenic gorge, to where the old railway ran until it was ripped up following the infamous Beeching purge.

Turn left and you come to the Warren, a public field open to the river and the Radnorshire hills. Turn right and you follow the bank to the new bridge, beyond which is the sewage works, where a stream trickles discreetly into the river by a small pebble beach. You can actually reach this place from a track at the other end of the town (turn left before the vets' clinic). There's a small car park, stepping down to green banks and the little beach and the mouth of the aforementioned humble stream. This is the Dulas Brook, far more important than it looks, because it marks the actual boundary between Wales and England, rushing down from a place called —

Cusop

A mysterious place in England, just. And although fields and the Dulas Brook divide them, well-wooded Cusop, with its big, dark houses, is virtually a suburb of Hay. King Richard's family home is here, and Herbert Rowse Armstrong, the famous Hay poisoner – the only solicitor ever actually hanged for murder, as the King likes to point out – also lived in Cusop.

It's a village without a centre, only a terminus with an ancient church and a castle mound and folklore involving fairies and the Will-o'-the-Wisp, retold by Mrs Leather, who wrote in 1912:

> Fairies have been seen dancing under foxgloves in Cusop
> Dingle within the memory of some now living there.

Top: Cusop Church. Bottom: part of the stone circle at the foot of Hay Bluff

Looking along the ridge of the Black Mountains above Hay (Hay Bluff is just off to the left)

I was interested in the Will-o'-the-Wisp, a moving light effect, often said to attract travellers from the road and into the abyss. Years earlier, our neighbour, Ken Ratcliffe, who came from Cusop, had told me about the time he saw the whole landscape inexplicably lit up. Ken's wife, Jessie thought it might have been a UFO. But unexplained phenomena are not uncommon in Cusop.

Its lower half, the fairy-haunted Cusop Dingle, has a road that follows the Dulas Brook along the England/ Wales border. Here, the brook is not the little stream that flows placidly into the big Wye by the Hay sewage works, but something more urgent and dramatic, with several waterfalls. The pool below one of the most dramatic of these, right next to the road, is deeper than it looks, and a man drowned there. Recently, since a car went over the edge, the pool has been caged by metal bars.

The low mound on which Cusop Castle stood is almost facing the church, which is partly Norman, possibly on the site of an earlier place of worship and is dedicated to St Mary. As is Hay Church. As is the little church up in the Black Mountains, beyond Hay Bluff, in the place called —

Above: the tiny church at Capel-y-ffin

Capel-y-ffin

The chapel at the end. But the end of what?

St Mary's, Capel-y-ffin is actually a very small church, endearingly bent, reached by the mountain road which passes under Hay Bluff, alongside a not very impressive but certainly well-appointed prehistoric stone circle.

Hay Bluff is where, in the 1980s, the Convoy used to gather in the autumn – a chain of ancient buses, vans and ex-ambulances carrying the post-hippies who came in search of the magic mushrooms growing in quantity around the Bluff. The key ingredient of these tiny fungi is psilocybin which can promote visionary experiences and has recently been described as better than Prozac, if less legal. A member of the Convoy once presented me with a bag of mushrooms which, he said, should be dried, crushed and brewed like tea, but I wimped out.

The Convoy were themselves a mixed bag, including romantics in search of a spiritual retreat, anarchists looking for a revolution and – let's not dress this up – a few itinerant thieves. New Age Travellers was the term they preferred, citing gypsy-rules when making yet another appearance at Talgarth Magistrates' Court, where they were represented by an amiable traveller who came into court wearing a black suit and carrying a stack of law books. He never really won, but it was fun

The ruins of Llanthony Priory in the Vale of Ewyas

while it lasted, and the Convoy slipped into history as part of a long tradition of eccentrics attracted to this corner of the Black Mountains.

Towards the end of the nineteenth century, the scattered farmers of Capel-y-ffin had watched, faintly baffled, as a band of robed monks arrived to build a monastery under the direction of a man seen by some as a living saint.

Joseph Leycester Lyne was an Anglican deacon, healer and visionary who had become obsessed with founding an Anglo-Catholic monastic community by refurbishing the scenic ruins of Llanthony Priory, lower down the valley. He'd toured Britain, raising the money through talks and healing sessions, but finally had to admit that modernising Llanthony was always going to be beyond him.

And so, under his working name of Father Ignatius, he switched his ambitions a few miles to a wooded hillside at Capel-y-ffin, a place whose wild, yet numinous qualities appealed to him at once. The neo-gothic monastery can be seen to this day, alongside Fr Iggy's church, which was not so well-built, and under which, eventually, he was buried, leaving the church to become a ruin.

Dismissed by many as a charlatan and exalted as an 'untiring sower of the seed divine' in the not entirely impartial biography by Beatrice, Baroness of

Opposite: the ruins of Llanthony Priory. Above left: the ruins of Father Ignatius' church. Above right: Capel-y-ffin monastery, now used as a Youth Hostel

Bertouche, Fr Ignatius was nationally famous in his day and is now virtually forgotten. His miracles – including the raising of a builder crushed to death by a pile of building stone – are regarded with a certain scepticism. Nonetheless, setting up a working monastery at a place like Capel-y-ffin was some achievement, and he did leave behind a mystery which puts the Black Mountains alongside Lourdes, Knock and Medjugorje.

THE LADY OF LLANTHONY

Beatrice de Bertouche is probably right when she says that, in a Catholic country, these phenomena would have been commemorated by 'some costly shrine'.

All we have at Capel is a touchingly-frayed modern statue of the Virgin Mary, now planted in front of Fr Iggy's monastery which has been used, of late, as a youth hostel and pony-trekking centre.

She's been moved, probably for her own safety, from the more exposed spot in a nearby field where, in the late summer of 1880, it all began to happen.

On the evening of Monday, 30 August, four choirboys were playing cricket, using a stick, in the Abbot's Meadow when one of them, John Stewart, 12, spotted what Beatrice describes as a dazzling figure gliding across the field.

> The form was of a woman, a veil hung over the head and face, the hands were both raised as if in blessing.

And, very slowly, it was coming towards them.

Thomas Foord, 11, was not happy about this.

'If it comes near me I'll hit it with my stick,' he's reported to have said.

THE KEYS TO THE KINGDOM

The Holy Mother, it seems, took the hint and slid into the hedge, where she remained for a few moments before vanishing into a bush.

And it was this bush which, on subsequent occasions, was seen to be lit up when the countryside all around was in darkness.

One of the monks, Brother Dunstan, was among the later witnesses.

> We knelt opposite the bush but some distance from it and began to say prayers and sing hymns but no figure appeared. Presently, I suggested that if it was really the Blessed Virgin who had appeared to the boys on Monday, possibly if we sang the Ave Maria she might again appear. So we began to sing the Ave ... and at once perceived the form of a woman surrounded by light at the top of the meadow by the gate.

The apparitions were said to have continued for some time, varying from full figures to starry lights in the bush, leaves from which would go on, according to Beatrice, to bring about 'miraculous cures'.

A small chorus of dissent was led by Sister Marry Agnes who, as a nun at Capel, had been badly bullied by a particular Mother Superior. Sister Marry Agnes suggested that the visitations had been created by a magic lantern, which, it has to be said, seems like a serious overestimation of the power of those early projectors.

Still, you can imagine that an appearance by the Virgin Mary might well have been dreamed up by Fr Ignatius as a way of attracting tourists and money; but, if international fame was expected, it didn't happen. The Lady of Llanthony has been all but forgotten. Far more has been written about the man who occupied the monastery in the 1920s, long after the departure of the monks.

Eric Gill, who came over from England, was a famous sculptor, stone carver and designer of typefaces. He was also a devout Catholic, of the Roman persuasion, who established at Capel-y-ffin a small community, including his extended family, the Welsh painter David Jones and various priests brought in to celebrate the Mass in his private chapel.

All very pre-hippy, but there was a darker side. A biography by Fiona McCarthy, published in 1989, revealed that Eric Gill's spiritual yearnings were coupled with physical desires of what you might call an experimental nature. He had sexual relations with his daughters. And his dog, apparently.

How Eric felt about the Lady of Llanthony doesn't seem to be recorded anywhere, but he fitted well into a pattern of unorthodox religious behaviour that I was beginning to detect in this area of the Border.

Figure of the Virgin Mary at Capel-y-ffin

Capel-y-ffin

It seemed not unreasonable to suggest, in *The Magus of Hay*, that another mystical community had existed near Capel-y-ffin in the 1980s, and that, because of its proximity to the town of books, it should attract some of the writers who increasingly converged on Hay.

An obvious one was the travel writer and novelist Bruce Chatwin, who spent a lot of time in the Black Mountains where he set his novel *On the Black Hill*. His fictional town of Rhulen – its name borrowed from a hamlet on the edge of Radnor Forest – is thought to have been based on Hay-on-Wye. Bruce Chatwin was a well-known freeloader, often borrowing people's houses to write in, notably Scethrog Tower, near Brecon, the fourteenth-century home of the jazz-singer, writer and journalist George Melly.

Jeremy Sandford, who wrote the seminal TV plays 'Cathy Come Home' and 'Edna the Inebriate Woman', lived in nearby Herefordshire, was a friend of the King of Hay, championed gypsies and travellers generally and wrote a book called *In Search of Magic Mushrooms*.

There's no record of the distinguished novelist Dame Beryl Bainbridge ever spending time at Capel-y-ffin, as she does in the novel, though it did seem the sort of thing she might do. I only met Beryl a couple of times – at the Hay Festival, as it happened – but she was always there in the background, since the days after my first novel, *Candlenight*, was discovered by her editor and friend, Anna Haycraft, who wrote as Alice Thomas Ellis. Dame Beryl's spiritual beliefs were uncertain, but her Anglo-Catholic funeral is legendary, and she just seemed to float naturally into *Magus*.

Meanwhile, down in Hay itself, the torch of Anglo-Catholicism had been reignited in the new millennium.

Mary's return

Capel-y-ffin, Llanthony, and eventually Abergavenny, are linked to Hay by the tortuous mountain road known as the Gospel Pass – so called because two prominent Apostles are said to have taken this route on a rare (extremely rare) visit to the British Isles.

Like the Malverns, which they face across Herefordshire, the Black Mountains have a long history of mysterious worship, Christian and pagan. But few people would have expected the air in Hay Church to be laden with the scent of incense again, so long after the Reformation.

Anglo-Catholicism has been a triumph for Father Richard Williams who, in an age of falling congregations, has more than tripled the turn-out at St Mary's. A tabernacle stands on the altar, guarded by a collection of candlelit figurines. Across from the votive stand is a painted Virgin and child. And the Mass is back. More Catholic, say some of the expanded flock, than most RC churches.

In the tradition of eccentricity without which Hay would be just another rural, market town, Fr Richard's curate was his standard poodle, Jimmy, who attended services along with any other dogs that happened to turn up with their owners.

It's the same at his other churches, at Llanigon and, of course Capel-y-ffin, about which Fr Richard wrote in his parish magazine:

> ... artists, poets and visionaries have found this place a place where 'Prayer is valid' ... where the veil between the visible world and the invisible has worn diaphanously thin.

Even Fr Richard is a little sceptical about some of the legends of Fr Ignatius, but he doesn't dismiss the sightings of the Lady of Llanthony. For him, too, the story is given a certain substance by the anecdote about the choirboy and the stick.

You may well be hearing more, sometime in the future, about the Virgin of the Black Mountains.

Hitler in the hills?

Fr Richard and Merrily Watkins are not in the same diocese, but neither Hereford nor Swansea-and-Brecon has a tradition of Anglo-Catholicism. Other ministers, in both dioceses, seem to take a dim view of what's happening in Hay. But, as we've seen, the Border country is good at breaking down barriers and making its own rules.

Also, there's always been a strong element of paganism in the border hills, some of it quite close to Christianity, as reflected by the Sheelagh-na-gig and green man ornaments in so many churches. But, at various times, there have also been signs of something radically opposed to Christianity, wilfully embracing shadows.

Nicholas Goodrick-Clarke's authoritative book, *Black Sun*, has a long chapter on extreme right-wing groups practising magic on the Welsh Border in the 1980s and '90s, and the Internet is still loaded with fascist philosophical ramblings by one or two people living around Herefordshire, Shropshire and Powys.

Goodrick-Clarke suggested these attitudes had formed out of the search for self-sufficiency which brought hundreds of good-lifers into the border hills in the 1970s. It's not difficult to imagine a few of them sharing the beliefs of the survivalists and white-supremacists in remote areas of the US. *Black Sun* suggests that Saxon and Nordic forms of paganism and the magical beliefs of Himmler's SS came together in areas of Herefordshire, Shropshire and Powys in the late twentieth century, with ceremonies at prehistoric sites and hints of blood sacrifice. The extent of this belief-system remains uncertain, but some of its followers – who regarded Hitler as an avatar or demi-god heralding a new era of violent ethnic cleansing in the West – do seem to be still around.

The family of William Joyce – the Nazi radio propagandist Lord Haw Haw – is said to have had links to Hay, and the Mosleyite Lord Brocket, apparently a guest at Hitler's birthday party, was up the road, for a time, at Kinnersley Castle. There were also rumours that the right-wing Lord Lucan was accommodated in the area while on the run following the murder of his children's nanny.

All far removed from the friendly, chaotic regime of Independent Hay, in Liberal-Democrat Brecon and Radnor, but everybody dreams, and some dreams are dark.

The future

The future for Hay is as blurred as the Lady of Llanthony.

A brain tumour caused a dramatic hiatus in Richard Booth's roller-coaster career and the progress of Independent Hay. He recovered, he's back ... but times have changed.

The Church of St Mary, Hay: exterior and chancel

The town is now well-established as an inland resort and tourist haven and the Castle, now in the hands of a local trust, is being revived as a centre for the arts. Richard's principal bookshop, The Limited, is in new hands, looks a good deal less eccentric, but is still trading as Richard Booth's Bookshop. But several second-hand bookshops, as well as the only purveyor of new books, have closed down in the past few years, victims of the Recession, the national decline of the high street and, of course, the rise of the e-book which means that far fewer books are now unobtainable and fewer people need to haunt the second-hand shops in search of some elusive title. Long-time bookseller Derek Addyman, who recently acceded to the title of Prince of Hay, declared war on the new devices, and the cover of *The Kindle Crack'd from Side to Side* by Agatha Addyman appeared in the window of the Murder and Mayhem bookshop.

There had been other tensions over the years: ambitious outsiders who wanted a piece of Hay, and – because Richard Booth wasn't really in charge – sometimes got one.

And success, too, had its inevitable downside for some people. Property prices went through the roof and local young people were forced out as wealthy incomers arrived, lured by the idea of a cultural haven in a comparatively remote area.

Again, this probably would not have happened if the King had possessed real power – Richard Booth made a point of employing local people and, as Gomer Parry points out, 'sometimes we even got paid'.

And some of the incomers were eccentric enough to fit in. I'm not going to name them; they know who they are. They're characters looking for a novel.

But, as you can't have too many real people in a novel, for *The Magus of Hay* I had to repopulate the town with a parallel cast of refugees who would fit the ethos. And if you find it hard to separate fact from fiction … you'll know you're finally starting to understand Hay.

14 A Deviant Burial

She stopped halfway up the hill. Turning to look back across the valley, she found she was viewing Cwmarrow Castle from a very different angle, the tower side-on so you could see that most of its back was missing, Like a movie-set castle, just a façade, impotent, relegated to the role of ornament. He don't like that, see, *local people would say.* He en't happy.

Friends of the Dusk

Cwmarrow Castle is hard to find. Snodhill Castle is a little easier. It's reached by some secret lanes in a fairly obscure part of Herefordshire's Golden Valley, and well worth a visit. And now, it seems, some local people want you to come.

You can get there, at last, in comparative safety. When *Friends of the Dusk* was being written, it wasn't easy to approach and, in the wrong weather, you might have had to be brought down on a stretcher. I first went in winter. No snow, but the access path was steep, overgrown and slippery as hell. There was also very little parking at the bottom of the hill on which it huddled in a tangle of trees.

It also seemed to be on private land, another reason I felt obliged to change the name and slightly alter the topography. But the main reason was that a small number of people do have to live in the immediate vicinity and not everybody wants to be linked with a haunt of the medieval undead.

Is it, really?

Well, Cwmarrow is, while Snodhill may not be. But I'd found a very old story and I needed a plausible location, and this obscure place had the right features.

Overleaf and page 130: Snodhill Castle

It seemed to be in the right general area, facing winds from Wales, and had a serious sense of the medieval about it.

Very little is known about the origins of Snodhill Castle, believed to date back to the days of King Stephen, who reigned not long after the Norman Conquest. It was said to have been one of the biggest early-Norman castles. In the sixteenth century it was apparently given by Queen Elizabeth I to her would-be (or perhaps it was more than that – see *The Bones of Avalon*) lover, Robert Dudley.

There are no records of it ever having been the home of Sir William Laudun, vampire slayer … but, then, no evidence that it wasn't.

THE MAP LEGACY

I always swore that this series would never go anywhere near werewolves, zombies, vampires or anything else bordering on fantasy. All right, maybe they seemed less like fantasy in parts of eastern Europe, but surely they were *just not British*.

Bram Stoker imported Dracula (from Transylvania to Whitby in Yorkshire) and Stephen King dumped another one in Maine. I had no intention of ever importing anything with fangs into the Welsh Border. But then I encountered Walter Map – scribe, cleric, historian and folklorist in the reign of Henry II – and found this wasn't necessary. Amazingly, we had what may well have been the first recorded story of a vindictive revenant.

Map (or Mapp) is a name still found in Herefordshire. Walter was definitely here in the twelfth century when he almost became Bishop of Hereford. But perhaps, if he had, he would have kept this story to himself.

It appears in his collection of tales *De Nugis Curialium* (*Trifles of the Courtiers* – Map spent time at the court of Henry II) which would, centuries later, be edited by none other than Montague Rhodes James, Provost of King's College, Cambridge who we met in *The Fabric of Sin*.

Monty was definitely the man for this tale of a knight, Sir William Laudun, who – probably in the second half of the twelfth century, according to Map – approached the then Bishop of Hereford, Gilbert Foliot, to ask for help with what remained of a certain Welshman, known for his evil nature, who

> 'died of late, unChristianly enough in my village and after four nights took to coming back every night to the village and will not desist from summoning, singly and by name, his fellow villagers who, upon being called, at once fall sick and die within three days, so that now there are very few of them left.'

Bishop Foliot seems to have known exactly how to deal with this: dig up the body, sever its neck with a spade, sprinkle the body and the grave with holy water, rebury.

Before the introduction of the wooden stake through the heart, this was one of the traditional methods of dealing with a vampire. The Bishop didn't use that word, of course, and there was no suggestion of puncture wounds and blood-sucking, but the essence of the vampire ethos is here, and Foliot saw it in terms of demonic possession. The man was evil and the evil lived on in his spirit, empowered and enhanced by the forces of darkness to re-enter and reanimate the body. To sustain itself, the entity would steal energy from the living, the victims selected and *summoned* by name.

THE SUMMONING

In some ways, the idea of a *summoner*, calling living people to their death, is even more sinister than the vampire legend, and takes us close to Snodhill Castle, which stands between the villages of Peterchurch and Dorstone.

Dorstone has a particularly scary story of a summoning. The tale, passed on by Mrs Leather in *The Folk-lore of Herefordshire*, relates to a locally-feared character known as Jack of France who found his nemesis in the village church.

> One night, the eve of All Souls, he was passing through the churchyard and saw a light shining in all the windows of the church. He looked in and saw a large congregation assembled, listening apparently to the preaching of a man in a monk's habit who was declaiming from the pulpit the names of all those who were to die during the coming year. The preacher lifted his head, and Jack saw under the cowl the features of the Prince of Darkness himself, and to his horror his own name given out among the list of those death should claim. He went home, and repenting too late of his evil deeds, took to his bed and died.

No blood-sucking involved in these summonings, but there's a definite malevolence here, all the more sinister for occurring in a church.

But let's conclude Walter Map's tale.

Basically, Bishop Foliot's instructions don't work. The evil runs too deep. The dead man continues to walk by night and prey on the villagers.

It's only when he gets round to Sir William himself, calling him out three times, that the evil spirit becomes vulnerable – not as much to holy water as cold steel.

Knowing now what he's dealing with, the knight springs out with his sword drawn, pursues the demon back to the grave and this time brings the sword down vertically on the head, slicing it in two down to the neck. Which seems to have worked. No more problems in the village. Vampire experts would say this was because iron, from which the sword was made, is also a constituent of blood.

But local people may have had a simpler way of dealing with a potential summoner, involving the symbolic silencing of the evil spirit. A number of early burials unearthed in recent years have revealed skeletons with the skulls detached and placed below the feet or, interestingly, with a stone wedged between the teeth. This is usually described as a *deviant burial*, with the suggestion that the internee was a notorious evil-doer and the body had been arranged to prevent it walking again, the stone hindering any summoning.

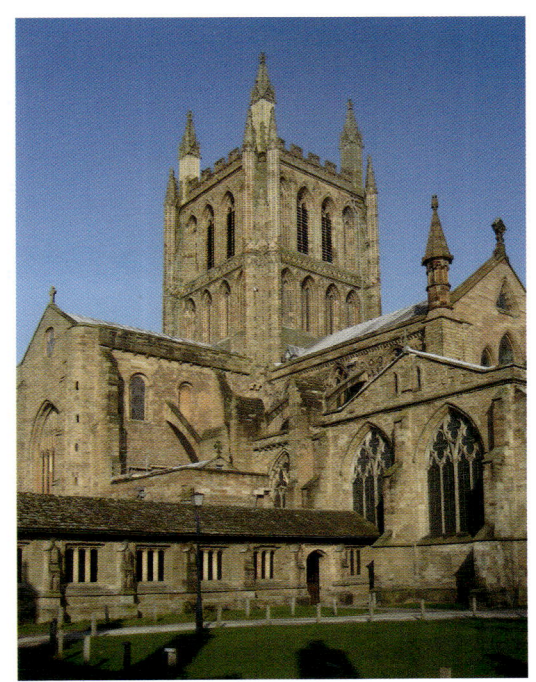

Hereford Cathedral

Hundreds of bodies have recently been excavated around Hereford Cathedral, where the contemporary Herefordshire storyteller David Phelps has suggested Gilbert Foliot ordered Laudun's vampire to be reburied. This looked like a suitable place for a deviant burial to be exposed, in *Friends of the Dusk*, during an autumn storm.

Of course, Walter might have made the whole thing up. But the fact that the story features an actual bishop, who was a fairly contemporary figure when *De Nugis Curialium* was written, suggests otherwise.

Ghost Villages

Walter Map says his story took place in Wales, and yet it's in Hereford Diocese. This is reasonable. Even today, areas of both Powys and Monmouthshire are in the diocese. Back in the twelfth century, much of what is now known as the Golden Valley would have been accepted as Wales and been largely Welsh-speaking. A Hereford man told me a few years ago that even when he was a boy, people used to refer to everywhere west of Clehonger as *Wales*.

What about the village?

Map doesn't identify the actual community, but this part of the Golden Valley again seems appropriate. There's no doubt that many villages in this area have disappeared since the Middle Ages – often, it's said, because the entire population was wiped out by plague and nobody wanted to move back into what was seen as a contaminated area. Often only the ruins of a castle – or, in most cases, just its mound – remain.

Today, a ruined castle somehow defines an area more than something better preserved. Even the earthworks retain a strong sense of mystery, strange and now untouchable in a farmer's field. The size of Snodhill Castle indicates that far more people lived in its medieval shadow than are there today.

In *Friends of the Dusk*, Jane spots the signs and fills in the fabric of a village that no longer exists.

It's surprising how many local people have never been to Snodhill. However, even as the book was being written, plans were being made to put it on the map. The Snodhill Castle Preservation Trust has been at work clearing the undergrowth, exposing forgotten walls and generally combatting nature's attempts to topple them.

It's already a revelation, and anyone can help by joining the Friends of Snodhill Castle.

Last word on vampires …

… comes, of course, from Ella Mary Leather, who reports her conversation with the daughter of a man at Weobley Marsh, who

> '… saw a strange creature come into his room one night, "something like a bat." His daughter told me it was one of the witches then living on the marsh. "But how did he know?" I asked. "He knocked the thing down with a handkerchief, and if it had been a bat he would have killed it for certain. But he lighted a candle after, and there was nothing there at all. You can't harm them folks."'

15 Dance the Darkness Down

The old year's hanging on a rusting hinge
Kids in the city on a drinking binge
And no-one hears the ancient engines
Grinding Underground.

Lol Robinson and Hazey Jane II
from *All of a Winter's Night*

St Lucy's night is the old New Year. It falls on 13 December, the time the Elizabethan poet John Donne called 'the year's midnight.'

It seemed appropriate that, in *All of a Winter's Night*, it should be celebrated in candlelight at the very exciting Kilpeck Church, with its saucy Sheelagh-na-gig, its posse of Green Men and dozens of magical images of medieval life.

The original importance of this little village church – why, in the middle of nowhere, it has more richly-decorated stonework than many cathedrals – remains a mystery.

Kilpeck Church is *all* mystery.

Why is it in such an immaculate state of preservation when the nearby Kilpeck Castle is a very sparse ruin?

Why does the stone itself seem to glow at sunset as if from within?

Is there a secret narrative in the frieze of stone corbels which looks like a petrified comic strip under the roof?

Overleaf: The Church of St Mary and St David, Kilpeck

Corbels on the eaves of Kilpeck Church

Why are so few of the images what we think of as obviously Christian? Serpents and dragons and other mythical beasts. Walls seething with images of good and evil, love and fear, angels and devils echoing laughter and screams.

The church of St Mary and St David remains the most perfect example of the Herefordshire School of Romanesque Sculpture. The church and the castle lie outside the comparatively-modern community of Kilpeck. The original village is visible only in bumps in the adjacent fields.

I've always found it a friendly place but the sense of *presence* is inescapable, the medieval energy seeping through the clunky Victorian embellishments.

In mid-May, 2011, 19 members of the British Society of Dowsers investigated the site with rods and pendulums, detecting underground flowing water, a spring under the altar, the possibility of a small stone circle having been where the nave is and what John Moss, who led the survey, described as a complex pattern of energies under the ancient font.

Many of the Kilpeck corbels seem curiously contemporary, like the dog and the rabbit (or hare and hound) cosying up to one another – the 'Disney corbel' as it's often called. The Sheelagh-na-gig, a woman comfortably exposing all, is found in many parts of Britain and Ireland, but Kilpeck's, with her lopsided smile, is probably the most famous. Don't ask me to explain this, but there's something very Herefordshire about her. She has a very important part (yes, possibly that part) to play in *All of a Winter's Night*.

> *The hunting tawny owl espies*
> *The dark between the Sheela's thighs*
> *But doesn't care to meet her eyes*
> *Till morning comes around*

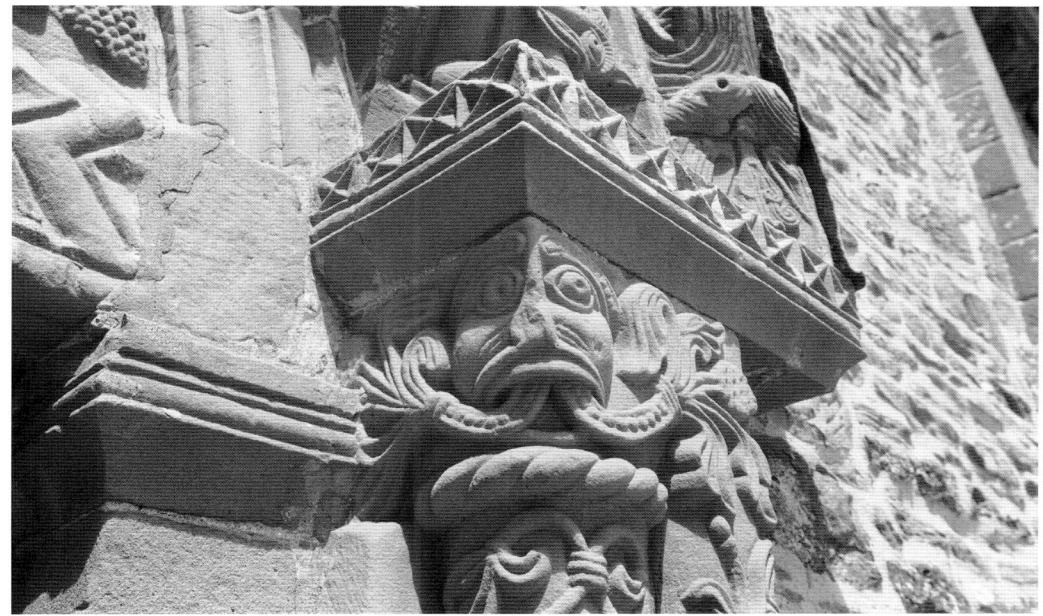

Green Man on the south doorway at Kilpeck Church

THE GREEN MAN

> *The farmer's poison spray pollutes*
> *The Green Man dines on twisted roots*
> *And all the land lies destitute*
> *The meadows turning brown*

We're not going on a full tour of the Kilpeck corbels here, because there are whole books that handle this in detail. But what does need to be mentioned is the veggie-faced creature who peers out from a high window facing the castle and, in stone, guards the spectacular south doorway with its great Norman arch.

The name Green Man as applied to a face framed by foliage dates back only to 1939 when it was invented by Lady Raglan to identify the one she'd found in her local church in Monmouthshire and several others in the area. Obviously it goes back many centuries before that and is often said to represent some pagan god or nature spirit.

In which case, why does it always turn up on Christian churches?

Nina Lyon travelled widely to uncover the Man's secrets in her book *Uprooted*, arriving, in the end, back at Kilpeck and the homes of neighbouring foliate friends, and exploring theories about what it might say about our relationship with the natural world.

All of a Winter's Night is the most agricultural of the Merrily Watkins novels, with feuding farmers and warnings of the endtime for some of Britain's most richly fertile fields.

What if the Green Man knows about the damage we might be doing to the land, as foretold in John Lewis Stempel's book *The Running Hare* which suggests we may only be 50 pesticide-fuelled harvests away from an agrarian apocalypse?

LORE OF THE DANCE

I always knew Kilpeck would provide a deep puzzle for Merrily but didn't want to 'loose her out' (as Gomer Parry would say) into this mysterious landscape, until it was part of something else, something bigger.

Which turned out also to include morris dancing.

During a fairly recent excavation in and around the ruins of Kilpeck Castle, archaeologists discovered a game much played in the Middle Ages: Nine Men's Morris. It was played in marked-out squares on turf, or a board or, as in this case, a stone. It's mentioned by Shakespeare and may date back to ancient Egypt. The movement of counters among concentric squares is said to reflect movements in morris dancing – often performed on village squares – and to have cosmic symbolism. I couldn't find any proof of this, but it did suggest to me that if people at Kilpeck Castle had played Nine Men's Morris, the village ought to have its own morris side.

Morris dancing has a long history in Herefordshire. Leominster Morris still flourishes and the Silurian side, based in Ledbury, was one of the first in modern times to perform what's become known as Welsh Border Morris.

Silurian's Welsh leader, the late Dave Jones, was convinced that Border Morris was far older than the less-aggressive Cotswold Morris and, with its phallic short sticks, had its roots in Celtic ritual and fertility dances.

The Fool, weaving in and out of the dance and its audience, is a feature of Border Morris, as is the Green Man. It was Phil Lister, former Green Man of Hereford's Breinton Morris who first suggested to me that the ancient dance would make a good theme for a Merrily novel.

Actually, this was just a reminder. Many years before, my old friend and mentor, the author Graham Nown, had given me copies of two articles from *The Enneagram*, journal of the followers of J.G. Bennett, who ran courses based on the teachings of G.I. Gurdjieff at Sherborne, Gloucestershire. Sherborne students were detecting similarities between the Morris and movements taught by Gurdjieff to alter human consciousness. These, in turn, had been developed from ancient Sufi and Dervish dances.

The remains of Kilpeck Castle

This made perfect sense to former Silurian Morris member Rob Elliott who writes in his inspiring book, *The Fool and his Dancers* about the transcendental side of the Border dance, often performed on key dates in the Celtic calendar.

'It was as if we had stepped out of this world and into another, slipping through the veil as it were. None of us could describe what had happened, but we all knew that something truly primal had taken place.'

Border Morris sides, particularly in Herefordshire and Shropshire, are traditionally all male and perform with their faces blackened, usually with a mixture of burnt cork and cider. It's been suggested that the first dancers were mainly farm-labourers who didn't want to be recognised when they performed on village squares to earn enough money to see their families through the winter months (and also pay for the beer and cider) when they weren't needed on the land.

What's been happening recently … well, you could see it coming.

Of late, the traditional blacking-up of Border Morris dancers has got them banned by some timid – and more than slightly dim – festival organisers, who see racism here, or think they ought to.

Which is even sillier than it sounds and threatens something that dancers like Rob Elliott perceive as a fundamental aspect of Border Morris.

'Above all,' he writes, 'the dancers need to set themselves apart whilst remaining part of their community … The dancers needed to be there but not there, human but not human. Originally, charred wood from the ceremonial fires would have done the job brilliantly, especially with the added significance of carbon (what we might call today bio-char) being a potent fertility conduit.'

A Border Morris revival was a feature of the folk-rock revolution in the 1970s, developed by the accordian ace John Kirkpatrick and the Shropshire Bedlams. If BM has always been the least socially-acceptable form of the dance, its condemnation by the politically-correct establishment of the early Third Millennium fits perfectly into its tradition.

Blacking up, as Rob Elliott says, concealed the features better than masks, as they danced-in the summer and the New Year. Danced to the sounds of drums and bells, to dispel evil spirits, demonstrating that they, too, could be scary… not least because their faces were hidden. In *All of a Winter's Night*, Lol Robinson sings,

> *The wind is prowling in the east*
> *To raise the devil, scorn the priest*
> *Let's light the lamps for Lucy's feast*
> *And dance the darkness down.*

16 Wanderer through the Woods

After a while, I thought I could hear the river. In my head. Like when you were a kid and you'd cup a seashell to your ear and listen to the sea. Back there, the river goes all twisty. Writhing back on itself. If you see it on a map it's almost making the shape of a shoe with a big heel, and then it's squirming away. It's over there … And back there … across the village. You can almost feel it, in front and coming up behind. The whole mood of the landscape is governed by the Wye.

The Fever of the World

The Wye is a complex river. No country owns it. It travels over 130 miles, in and out of Wales and England, sometimes serene, sometimes sinister. It captures hearts and takes lives.

Beginning as a trickle up at Plynlimon, a high, remote area of Mid-Wales, it passes by Welsh country towns – Rhayader, Builth, Hay. But its first and last city is Hereford, after which, it moves towards the dramatic area termed 'Wye Valley' in holiday guides.

This part of the lower Wye was in at the birth of the word 'picturesque', when Britain's first tourists cruised through placid water meadows into sometimes forbidding woodland and under possibly-hostile rocks, past castles and churches, through history into prehistory and places that only exist in legend.

This is where Herefordshire merges with Gloucestershire and Monmouthshire, the river doubling back on itself, as if trying to catch its own tail, its banks breeding forestry and its high cliffs housing birds of prey.

The Wye near Symonds Yat

This is where the effects of the wild weather from up around the source are felt. Seventy miles downriver in pastoral Ross-on-Wye, you'll sometimes find severe flooding on a warm day under an empty blue sky.

The lower Wye pays for its famous beauty, and so, occasionally, do people. It's said the river takes a sacrifice every year, and most of them have been at this end, where small boats are launched and sometimes capsize, and climbers tumble from the towers of rock.

Memories, good, bad and inspirational, are made here. The painters take sketches, the poets take notes. Famous painters – J.M.W. Turner, Samuel Palmer. And famous poets, like William Wordsworth, whose life and senses may have been altered here.

WORDSWORTH'S WYE

> *O sylvan Wye! Thou wanderer through the woods*
> *How often has my spirit turned to thee.*
>
> From *Lines composed a few miles above Tintern Abbey,*
> *on revisiting the banks of the Wye during a tour.*

Tintern Abbey is never mentioned in Wordsworth's celebrated poem, which is usually known just as *Tintern Abbey*. In fact, the abbey only appears in the title as a reference-point – these are the best-known ruins on the banks of the Wye. In the end, the poem is a hymn to a river that seeps into the soul.

In 1792, still in his early twenties, Wordsworth returned from a period in France, leaving there a girlfriend, Annette Vallon and a baby daughter. He'd had to get out of France because of the war that had begun with England. Already disillusioned by the Revolution he'd once supported, he was entering a period of uncertainty about his future.

With no prospect of a decent job, he joined a wealthier friend, William Calvert on a tour of the West, destined to end in North Wales.

Unfortunately – or perhaps not – their *whiskey*, a light carriage drawn by a single horse, had to be abandoned after it was damaged on Salisbury Plain. Calvert took off on the horse, leaving Wordsworth to rely on what his sister Dorothy called his 'firm friends – a pair of stout legs.' Which was how he subsequently wound up alone in the Wye Valley where, according to his biographer, Mary Moorman, 'his genius was fully realised.'

We know more about his return to the valley five years later, accompanied by Dorothy, when he wrote *Tintern Abbey*.

Which is misleading. All the evidence points to it being composed – and about – somewhere more than a few miles up-river. A place that he hardly went out of his way to identify. Several episodes seem to relate to his first visit. In the year 2000, David Miall, of the University of Alberta, tracked down the poem's probable location to somewhere 17 miles upriver from Tintern.

> *The sounding cataract ... the tall rock ... the deep and gloomy wood*

These and other elements seem to point at Symonds Yat – specifically Yat Rock and the noisy New Weir (the full case for Symonds Yat can be found online in the article *Locating Wordsworth*).

It's clear that something profound happened to Wordsworth on that first troubled journey up the valley, which he dwelled on during his second walk, with Dorothy, five years later.

Essentially, it looks as if the Wye awoke the poet to another level of consciousness, entering a 'serene and blessed' state where

> *… we are laid asleep*
> *In body, and become a living soul*
> *While with an eye made quiet by the power*
> *Of harmony, and the deep power of joy,*
> *We see into the life of things.*

The valley, which led him into Wales via Hay-on-Wye, became a spiritual refuge for Wordsworth, its atmosphere and images living inside his head, in a place of meditation.

> *Oft in lonely rooms and 'mid the din,*
> *Of towns and cities, I have owed to them,*
> *in hours of weariness sensations sweet,*
> *Felt in the blood and felt along the heart;*
> *And passing even into my purer mind.*

The Stone and the Wicker Man

Salisbury Plain, where the whiskey mishap threw Wordsworth into solitude, was fateful in other ways. Here, in full light of day, within sight of Stonehenge, his mind was invaded by what Mary Moorman calls 'daydreams of the savagery of prehistoric man' - human sacrifices performed by druids using a wicker man. Imaginary scenes, probably conditioned by his experiences in revolutionary France, because he'd been drawn to the druids with their cosmic knowledge and stone circles.

Wordsworth had always loved old stone monuments and longed to uncover their meaning. *Speak, Giant-mother! tell it to the Morn*, he cried out to his native Cumbria's Long Meg.

On Salisbury Plain he seem to have been overcome with fear, says Moorman.

Hard to imagine, though, that this fear would have made him avoid prehistoric monuments from then on.

Really hard to imagine that, while visiting Symonds Yat and the neighbouring village of Goodrich, with its famous medieval castle, he totally failed to notice the Queen Stone. Although he might today.

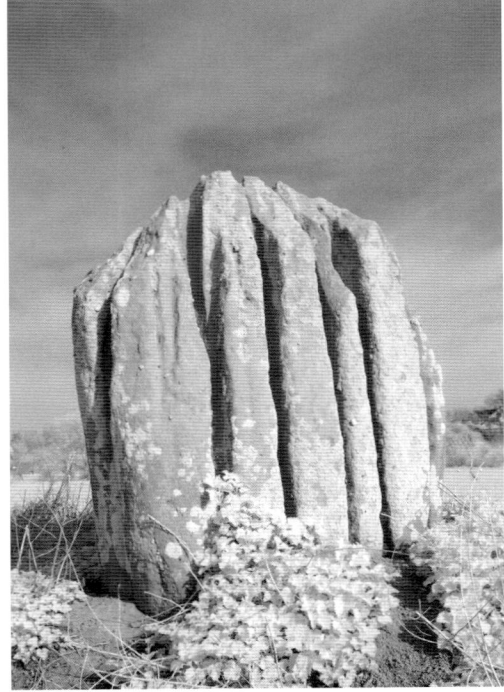

The Queen Stone, including (at top) Alfred Watkins demonstrating his Wicker Man in c.1933 (NB The Queen Stone stands on private land and is not publicly accessible)

I realise that modern-day ley-hunters, prehistorians and practising pagans must resent the fact that the biggest standing stone in Herefordshire is on private land and not available to view, touch, or use to support a picnic lunch. But, in some odd way, I like that.

The owner of the land on which the Queen Stone stands is quoted on the internet as not wanting 'hippies howling at the moon.' I can understand that. If I had land with a standing stone on it, I might not be too happy about awakening at night to the sound of chanting.

Still, it's interesting, because an ex-soldier, who's visited hundreds of ancient stones, told me that this was the one site he definitely wouldn't want to spend a night at. Very sinister, he said. Very powerful.

The Queen Stone is sunk into a field near the top of a horseshoe bend in the Wye between Goodrich and Symonds Yat East. More than half of it is under the ground. Above, it's about six feet tall but also chunky and has deep grooves in it. The grooves could be natural but we know they don't continue below ground level because of an archaeological excavation in 1926 by Alfred Watkins, photographer, antiquary and discoverer of leys.

He it was who suggested the sandstone monument had been a sacrificial stone. I'm not sure whether he ever actually said the grooves had been made to channel victims' blood into the ground to promote fertility, but it makes you think.

Or was the victim burned, either dead or alive, on top of the Queen Stone? There's a photograph of Mr Watkins conducting one of his open-air lectures, at the stone, for a large number of followers. On top of the stone is a cage of branches supported by rods placed in the grooves. Viewed along one of the alignments he believed emanated from the stone, the blaze would have been like a beacon.

Yes, we're talking about a wicker man, as used – according to the Romans – by druids. This one was certainly big enough for at least one human victim, and fragments of burned bone were found during Mr Watkins's excavation.

I've seen the Queen Stone from a distance – how long a distance I refuse to say. But it was on a winter's evening, just before nightfall, and I admit to experiencing a certain dark excitement which could only have been enhanced by the barbed wire and keep-out signs.

I was thinking about those howling hippies. Maybe the landowner was doing it for their own good.

For the Queen Stone is part of an alignment that perhaps does more than illustrate Alfred Watkins's theory of leys.

The Church of St Dubricius, Symonds Yat

The Timeline
(1) Saint Dubricius

Mr Watkins said he'd found three leys involving the Queen Stone. I could only find this one, with a possible six points. It's not exactly an orthodox alignment – it may not qualify as a ley at all, as you won't be able to walk it unless, as Jane Watkins observes in the novel, you're in possession of Christ-like skills or carrying a coracle, because it crosses the River Wye at least four times. It is, in fact, a perfect timeline which, in a very short distance, brings together the history and key legends of the lower Wye Valley.

If you follow the line, you'll be walking in a south-westerly direction down the horseshoe made by the Wye and then paddling your coracle across to a small church on the opposite bank. You might even come ashore at the old landing stage. At one time, this was how many worshippers arrived at the Church of St Dubricius, which is so close to the Wye that, as the vicar, Kevin Cecil says, a funeral conducted when the river's in flood can look like a burial at sea. All entirely appropriate because St Dubricius is a figure who links history with legend.

First, the history. Dubricius – Dyfrig in Welsh – has no known birthday, but died around the year 550 on the island of saints, Bardsey, off the North Wales coast. His mother was the daughter of a chieftain in South Herefordshire, where

WANDERER THROUGH THE WOODS 149

several ancient churches carry his name and where, as one of the most learned Celtic bishops, he founded the monastery of Hentland. Dubricius's name is also found in Somerset on the other side of the Bristol Channel. He ordained another notable bishop, Samson, described by an early (possibly seventh-century) biographer as a magician who had second sight.

Which leads us nicely into the legend, which explains why Dubricius is seen as the patron saint of the Wye.

The story begins before his birth with his grandfather, Peibio, the 'king' or chief of Ergyng (Archenfield) who, on discovering that his daughter, Efryddil, is about to become a single mother, has her put in a sack and thrown into the river. When she fails to drown, he decides to have her burned alive on a pyre of logs. Somehow, this doesn't work either and, the next we hear, Efryddil and her baby, Dyfrig/ Dubricius, are both doing well at Madley, between Hereford and the Black Mountains. Efryddil marries the baby's father, and relations are re-established with Peibio, who's so impressed by miracles worked by his grandson that he's glad to see the boy entering the Church. It seems to have been a fast-track clerical career which included the baptism of Arthur.

Yes, *that* Arthur.

The Timeline
(II) Caves

Mary Andere's *Arthurian links with Hereford* covers the full story, which is fascinating but doesn't really have a part to play in this novel. Whether or not the fifth- or sixth-century leader who is the 'historical' King Arthur actually functioned in this area, it does lead us to the rather sinister wooded hill known as the Doward.

The church of St Dubricius is in the parish of Whitchurch, although it's actually on the edge of what's known as Symonds Yat West which, with its caravan site, electronic amusement hall, riverside bar and, in summer, a big wheel known as The Wye Eye, is Hereford's only 'modern' holiday resort.

The Doward broods over it.

With its steep, narrow, overgrown lanes, the Doward, especially in winter, feels like a direct route to the heart of the Dark Ages.

There are actually two hills, Little Doward and Great Doward, both rich in minerals and history. The ancient British leader Vortigern is said to have died here, where there are traces of a hill fort and other earthworks. Dark lanes give way to forestry tracks leading down to the Wye and the Biblins suspension footbridge.

And to King Arthur's cave.

Opposite: King Arthur's Cave

Actually there are a number of caves sunk into the Little Doward above the Seven Sisters rocks, which overlook the Wye. They can be reached by a turning signposted to The Doward from the hamlet of Crocker's Ash. If you pull into a very small parking area on the right, a rutted footpath takes you down, past a quarry, to the caves.

Perhaps the one with the double entrance, near the end of the row, was called King Arthur's Cave because of the outsize human skeleton supposed to have been found there a few hundred years ago, taken away apparently for shipping to America and then somehow lost.

Several of the caves down here have sheltered 'rooms' which clearly served as Stone Age homes. The remains of

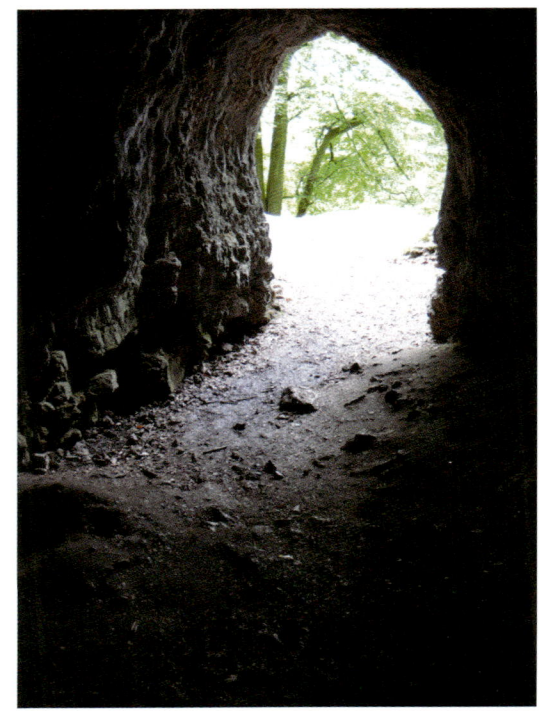

King Arthur's Cave

animals including mammoth, hyena and woolly rhino were found here, along with flint artefacts and evidence of fires in the entrances.

Has the cave had more recent occupancy? Dr David Miall suggested that this might be the one mentioned by Wordsworth in *Tintern Abbey*, the …

> … *hermit's cave, where by his fire*
> *The hermit sits alone.*

I was told that this immediate area was well-used for pagan rituals, but it was suggested that the circle of small stones we found not far from King Arthur's cave might just be a relic of a recent Arthurian feature film shot around the cave. But there may have been ritual stones here, which would explain its alignment, through both Dowards, with the Queen Stone and the Church of St Dubricius, which is certainly old enough to have been built on an ancient pagan site.

The ley proceeds down through the Seven Sisters rocks and across the Wye where it appears to end at Far Hearkening Rock, apparently a natural formation famous for its acoustics. A gamekeeper could stand here, it was said, and detect the sounds of poachers moving around.

The Timeline
(III) Goodrich Court

As you head north-east along the line from the Queen Stone, over the river again, through the Goodrich crossroads, now including the A40, you emerge not in the precincts of the medieval Goodrich Castle, but some distance to the west where another castle once stood. You can still see its turreted sandstone gatehouse on the edge of the A40 as you drive down from Ross to Monmouth.

This well-preserved edifice is all that remains of Goodrich Court, built in 1828 by the wealthy lawyer and antiquary Sir Samuel Rush Meyrick after the owners of the Goodrich Castle ruins refused to sell them to him.

Meyrick, who had come from North Herefordshire via London, wanted to restore the castle as a museum for his huge collection of armour and weaponry, medieval and earlier. Goodrich Court, with its fairytale pinnacles, was far more visible, as it was intended to be, to the new tourists cruising downriver towards an equally fantastical landscape, who then would disembark for the guided tour.

The gatehouse of Goodrich Court, with the A40 passing in front

But Meyrick didn't stop there. Turning to the secluded village of Goodrich, he and his architect, Edward Blore, looked around for what else they could medievalise. The pub, now called Ye Hostelrie, was given turrets and a steep, Gothic window. It's somehow aged into its role and now looks quite atmospheric.

But after Meyrick's death, the days of Goodrich Court itself were numbered. The armour and furnishings were sold and the Court's last meaningful function was as a refuge for the staff and pupils of a private school in Essex during the Second World War. As the twentieth century entered its second half, the building was demolished. Now the gatehouse guards empty fields.

William Wordsworth would have approved – a fitting end to what he'd described as 'Meyrick's impertinent structure.'

Whether he ever met Meyrick is not known. They did have a certain amount in common, including an interest in druids, who were generally seen at the time, because of Roman propaganda, as the most barbaric form of heathen. Did Meyrick ever attempt to buy the land on which the Queen Stone sits, down near the river at Goodrich? I can't see that he wouldn't have put in an offer for it.

And how could Wordsworth have failed to check out the stone while visiting Goodrich, whose castle drew him back after 50 years, in the hope of meeting there again the mysterious person who appears in one of his most enigmatic poems.

You may already know about this curious encounter. But if not, you might prefer to save the details for the novel, *The Fever of the World*.

Goodrich Castle

17 The Others

Lying low, at the centre of the well-tamed land, snug as a ground-nesting bird, was this bright and modern country settlement, its buildings elegantly structured with red brick and new timber framing. I marked a proud, towered church with a flag of St George. And sensed a glow about the place ...

The Heresy of Dr Dee

When Jack went to ring the old bell, he walked alone. Nobody else on the streets, the town holding its breath, even the sagging old buildings seeming to tense their timbers.

Curfew

Actually, before this was Merrily's Border, it was Gomer Parry country. And before that – four centuries before – it was Dee country.

Gomer made his first appearance in 1992, in my second novel, *Crybbe*, now republished as *Curfew*.

Looking back, this was quite an influential story. It was, to be honest, designed as a British answer to Stephen King, who has, over the years, inflicted all kinds of alien horrors on the US state of Maine, where he lives, prompting several other American writers to import elements of English and Welsh folklore into the New World. Occasionally, it worked. More often than not it made you wince.

So *Curfew* brings together many of the mysteries – British mysteries, *in situ* – relating to prehistoric monuments, mainly standing stones, circles and burial mounds. It's the story of a small town on the Welsh Border chosen as a centre for New Age research by an Australian entrepreneur who wants to restore the ancient stones that once surrounded it and falls foul of local people who know things he doesn't.

There isn't, as far as I know, a town anywhere in Radnor or Herefordshire that was ever inside a stone circle, in the way of, say, the village of Avebury, in Wiltshire. But most of *Crybbe's* other peculiarities were drawn from established legends and real features, notably —

THE CURFEW

Crybbe is not entirely based on Presteigne – think also Knighton, Bishops Castle and Clun – but, well, mostly it is.

Presteigne, though in Wales and once the county town of Radnorshire, lies on the English side of the border earthwork Offa's Dyke. With its crooked timber-framed buildings and medieval air, it seems very olde English, sometimes *merrie*, sometimes less so.

This is the town with the curfew, established in 1565 by John Beddoes, the Elizabethan wool merchant after whom the local high school would be named. The curfew bell is in the tower of the parish church, and a sum of money – the income from the lease of local fields – was left by John Beddoes to ensure that it would always be rung every night.

When, some years ago, its future was threatened, the musician Mike Oldfield who lived near Kington for some years, stepped in with the money. The fact that music from Oldfield's *Tubular Bells* had been the theme of *The Exorcist* did not go unnoticed – well, not by me, anyway.

The story retold in *Curfew*, about a dark force in the form of a hound coming down from an ancient mound into the town, echoes an experience related, in a radio programme I made, by the licensee of a pub in Presteigne who was terrified by a howling at the bottom of the stairs in the night, when there was nothing there. She said her own West Highland terrier had, uncharacteristically, hidden under the bed. There were also fears that a previous landlady, who died after an unexplained fall from an upstairs window, had wanted to make an urgent exit from the premises at night.

There are, of course, other strange stories in Presteigne, where, during the 1980s, the resident policeman was also the local wart-charmer. It makes perfect sense that the family of a famous Elizabethan astrologer and magician should have lived not far away.

DR DEE

Of all the Elizabethan heroes, John Dee is the most undersung. Recognised all over Europe as a brilliant mathematician by his early twenties, his reputation in

Presteigne Church

Britain has always been discoloured by his experiments with magic.

Magic, of course, is what science used to be called in the days when it was linked with religion. John Dee sought to chart the dimensions of creation and know the mind of God – nothing too ambitious. His friend and former pupil, Robert Dudley, later Earl of Leicester, asked him to forecast a fortuitous day for the coronation of the new queen, which he did, and was consulted by her on matters of the Hidden for the rest of her long reign. Unlike Drake, Raleigh & Co., however, he was never given a title and never made much money.

John was born in London, his father, Rowland Dee, having moved there from the family home, Nant-y-groes, near Pilleth, a few miles out of Presteigne.

The Heresy of Dr Dee takes John back to his roots in search of the Wigmore Shewstone, a famous crystal through which he believed he might catch celestial rays and raise his own consciousness to a level which could allow him to communicate with angelic forces. Which, in those days, was very much science.

The shewstone is based on an actual crystal which, for some time, was owned by the Harley family of Brampton Bryan. Nobody seems to know where it is now, but the Dee home, Nant-y-groes, can certainly still be seen. There are two houses there now: a farmhouse and a larger dwelling, expanded in Victorian times, on the other side of the lane from Whitton.

Both face Pilleth Hill, site of the battle in which a couple of thousand English soldiers were slain by the army of Owain Glyndwr and his general Rhys Gethin. Bones of the victims were still turning up on the hill in recent years, and memories of it were still painfully fresh in the 1560s when, in *The Heresy of Dr Dee*, Dee and Dudley arrive in Presteigne. Pilleth Church, which overlooks the novel's bloody climax, was burned down by the Welsh, then rebuilt and now has a strangely cheerful air. It was here, allegedly, that John's grandfather, Bedo Dee, had his son baptised in wine.

Pilleth Church

At Wigmore Abbey I discovered Abbot John Smart, a notorious wheeler-dealer who would undoubtedly have got along well with the renowned TV secondhand car dealer, Ambrose Boyce, as played by John Challis, who now lives there. It was John and his wife Carol who introduced me to Smart, who was involved in sundry fiddles and property deals and was not big on chastity. A man just demanding to be in the novel, so he is.

The classic portrait of John Dee and the younger man 'exposed' by Bev Craven

Although John Dee never makes it to Wigmore in *Heresy*, he actually did find his way there about ten years later to search the remains of Wigmore Castle for old books and documents to add to his famous library. Dee's diaries – at least the ones that have been found – make no mention of him returning to his family home, but it seems unlikely that he didn't. And there's a period, during his early 30s, when his biographers have been unable to discover what he was up to. It seemed reasonable for me to try and fill in the gaps, with reference to what was happening in England at the time.

But what did John Dee look like in those days? The only portraits show him as middle-aged or elderly, and these have tended to condition the public perception of him as an old wizard, maybe Head of Maths at Hogwarts. I needed a picture of a younger man to work with, so I asked the graphic designer Bev Craven if he could take the most famous portrait of Dee, darken the hair, lose the white beard and ... well, here he is at 33, still a little wary, even paranoid, but then he had cause to be.

December ...

... the other novel set on the Welsh Border, takes us back to Llanthony Priory, the medieval monastery which Fr Ignatius could never afford to restore.

This scenic ruin at the southern end of the Black Mountains was the model for the sinister abbey of Ystrad Ddu (every stone cemented in blood) in a story which turned the small hotel built into one corner of the ruins into a recording studio.

In December, a group of musicians falls victim to bad things linked to the famous Christmas massacre at Abergavenny Castle perpetrated by the Norman baron William de Braose (also of Hay Castle fame) in a bid to suppress Welsh opposition. The novel expands the legend of the harp-player who was supposed to have escaped the massacre and, for reasons too complicated to explain here, introduces the spectre of John Lennon. It also involves the Skirrid, the cleft peak near Abergavenny and one of the key turrets on the ramparts of the Hereford skyline, which is said to have split at the moment Jesus Christ died on the cross.

The novel was out of print for several years but is now back in a new paperback from Corvus and an illustrated collector's edition from MHB.

There's also a full-length CD of music recorded at the Abbey by the band Philosopher's Stone, and remixed by Allan Watson, which takes the story a stage further. *Abbey Tapes, the Exorcism* is available through the website www.philrickman.co.uk. A full-length *December* audiobook read by Sean Barrett and including snatches of the music, is available from Isis.

Anna Maxwell Martin as Merrily Watkins with David Threlfall as Huw Owen in the ITV Studios television adaptation of Midwinter of the Spirit *(2015)*

The Merrily Watkins Series (So Far) with Principal Locations

The Wine of Angels (1998)	Ledwardine
Midwinter of the Spirit (1999)	Hereford
A Crown of Lights (2001)	The Radnor Valley
The Cure of Souls (2001)	The Frome Valley
The Lamp of the Wicked (2002)	Ross-on-Wye & the Forest of Dean
The Prayer of the Night Shepherd (2004)	Kington
The Smile of a Ghost (2005)	Ludlow
The Remains of an Altar (2006)	The Malverns
The Fabric of Sin (2007)	Garway
To Dream of the Dead (2008)	Ledwardine, Hereford
The Secrets of Pain (2011)	Hereford and Brinsop
The Magus of Hay (2013)	Hay-on-Wye
The House of Susan Lulham (2014)	Hereford
Friends of the Dusk (2015)	Golden Valley
All of a Winter's Night (2017)	Kilpeck
The Fever of the World (2021)	Lower Wye Valley

Also available are two full-length CDs: *Songs from Lucy's Cottage* and *A Message from the Morning,* by Lol Robinson with Hazey Jane II. A third relates to *December: Abbey Tapes, the Exorcism,* produced by Prof. Levin from the Abbey sessions. All available through the website, www.philrickman.co.uk and from iTunes.

Select Bibliography

Mary Andere, *Arthurian Links with Herefordshire* (Logaston Press)
Richard Booth, *My Kingdom of Books* (Y Lolfa)
Mark Bowden, with David Field & Helen Winton, *The Malvern Hills, An Ancient Landscape* (English Heritage)
Paul Broadhurst, *The Green Man and the Dragon* (Mythos)
Bromyard and District Local History Society, *A Pocketful of Hops*
Ronald Bryer, *Not the Least, The Story of Little Malvern* (The Self-publishing Association)
Brian Cave, *The Countryside around Weston and Lea* (The Forest Bookshop)
Kate Clarke, *The Book of Hay* (Logaston Press)
Frank Collins, *Baptism of Fire* (Corgi)
Michael Cox, *M.R. James, An Informal Portrait* (Oxford)
    (Also strongly recommended: *The Ghosts and Scholars* magazine and online, edited by Rosemary Pardoe)
Paul Devereux, *Spirit Roads* (Collins & Brown)
        — *Haunted Land* (Piatkus)
Rob Elliott, *The Fool and his Dancers* (Elliott)
Tony Geraghty, *Who Dares Wins* (Warner books)
Richard Gravil, *Wordsworth's Bardic Vocation, 1787–1842* (HEB)
Richard Hayman, *Wye* (Logaston Press)
Pat Hughes and Heather Hurley, *The Story of Ross* (Logaston Press)
Ronald Hutton, *Blood and Mistletoe* (Yale)
Michael Kennedy, *The Life of Elgar* (Cambridge)
    (Also worth getting hold of Ken Russell's early BBC documentary on Elgar)
Ella Mary Leather, *The Folk-lore of Herefordshire* (Logaston Press)
Patrick Jasper Lee, *We Borrow the Earth* (Thorsons)
David Lloyd, *The Concise History of Ludlow* (Merlin Unwin)
Rosalind Lowe, *Sir Samuel Meyrick and Goodrich Court* (Logaston Press)
Les Lumsdon, *A Guide to Slow Travel in the Marches* (Logaston Press)
Nina Lyon, *Uprooted* (Faber)
Edmund J. Mason, *The Wye Valley* (Hale)
John Michell, *The View over Atlantis* (Garnstone, Abacus)
        — *The New View over Atlantis* (Thames & Hudson)
        — *City of Revelation* (Abacus)
Mary Moorman, *William Wordsworth, Early Years* (Oxford)

Jerrold Northrop Moore, *Elgar, Child of Dreams* (Faber)
Roy Palmer, *Herefordshire Folklore* (Logaston Press)
    — *The Folklore of Radnorshire* (Logaston Press)
    — *The Folklore of (old) Monmouthshire* (Logaston Press)
Huw Parsons, *Planet Hay* (Peevish Bee Books)
George Peterken, *Wye Valley* (Collins)
Susan Peterken, *Landscapes of the Wye Tour* (Logaston Press)
Stuart Piggott, *The Druids* (Thames & Hudson)
Tamzin Powell, *The Witches Ways in the Welsh Borders* (Airheart)
Graham Roberts, *Around & About Herefordshire and the Southern Marches* (Logaston Press)
Ward Rutherford, *The Druids and their Heritage* (Gordon & Cremonesi)
Ron Shoesmith, *Alfred Watkins – a Herefordshire Man* (Logaston Press)
    — and Andy Johnson (editors) *Ludlow Castle* (Logaston Press)
Fred Slater, *The Nature of Central Wales* (Barracuda)
Rob Soldat, *A Walk around Hay* (Marches Vade Mecum)
Audrey Tapper, *Knights Templar and Hospitaller in Herefordshire* (Logaston Press)
Joan and Brian Thomas (and others), *Garway Hill Through the Ages* (Logaston Press)
Malcolm Thurlby, *The Herefordshire School of Romanesque Sculpture* (Logaston Press)
Thomas Traherne, *Selected Poems and Prose,* ed. Alan Bradford (Penguin)
Alfred Watkins, *Alfred Watkins' Herefordshire*, with Introduction by Ron and Jennifer Shoesmith (Logaston Press)
    — *The Old Straight Track* (Abacus)

Index

Addyman, Derek 126
Ariconium 52
Armstrong, Herbert Rowse 113
Arthur, King 150
    Cave 150–152
    Stone 93
Avenbury Church 36–38

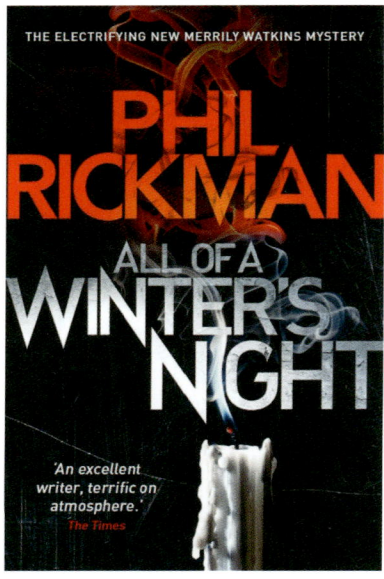

Baskerville, family 57–59
    Harry 54
    Sir Henry 53
    Sir Hugo 53, 56
    Ralph Hopton 57
Thomas Baskerville Mynors 57
Baskerville Hall 57–59
Beddoes, John 156
Black Dai 49
Black Vaughan 54, 55, 57, 59
Booth, Richard 107–108, 111, 124, 126
Boswell, Al 44
Bredwardine Bridge vii
Brinsop Court 96, 97, 101, 106
    Church 96, 97, 101–103
    Dragon's Well 101
British Camp 69–71, 74
British Society of Dowsers 25, 70, 138

Brocket, Lord 124
Buckland, Victoria 99
Burn, Gordon 46

Cabell, Sir Richard 54
Calvert, William 145
Capel-y-ffin 17, 116–122
    monastery 117, 119
Cascob Church 33, 35
    abracadabra charm 35
Castell Crugeryr 31, 33
Cave, Brian 52
Chatwin, Bruce 122
cider 5–14, 142
Clehonger 133
Coggan, Archbishop Donald 15
Collins, Frank 100
Comber, Sir William 101, 106
Conan Doyle, Arthur 2, 53, 54, 57–60
    Georgina 57
    Louise 57
Coughton Valley 49
Credenhill 11, 12, 95, 99, 101
    Church 12, 105
    Hillfort 98
Cusop 112–115
Cwmarrow Castle 127

de Braose family 111, 160
de Dinan, Joce 62, 63
de la Bere family 58
de la Bruyere, Marion 62, 63
de Lacy family 63
de Lisle, Arnold 63
de Molay, Jacques 81, 83, 84
Dee, Dr John 155–159
deliverance 14–21, 44, 50, 70,
Denny, Tom 12
Devenish, Lucy 8, 10, 11, 13, 14
Devereux, Paul 25
Didlick, Mr J. 63, 64
Dilwyn 5, 29
Dinedor Hillfort 23–26, 29, 88, 89, 92, 101
    Serpent 26, 87–89, 92
Discoed Church 33

Dobbs, Canon Thomas 21
Donne, John 135
Dore Abbey 78, 79
Dorstone 93, 132
dragons 31, 59, 138
Dragon's Back, The 34
Drake, Nick 13, 14, 92
Dulas Brook 113, 115
Dunfield Manor 60

Eardisland 5
Eardisley 10, 57
Ednol Church 36, 37
Efryddil 150
Elgar, Sir Edward 2, 72–76
    Caractacus 74–75
    Cello Concerto 74
    Dream of Gerontius 76
Elliott, Rob 142
Ergyng (Archenfield) 150
exorcism – see deliverance

Foliot, Bishop Gilbert 131–133
folklore (see also Black Vaughan; Leather, Mary Ella) 1, 9, 10, 39, 45, 59, 77, 111, 113, 155

Forest of Dean vii, 45, 52
Fortune, Dion 25
Four Stones, The 32, 33
Frome Valley 36, 39–41

Garway 19, 77–85
    Church 19, 77, 80–84
        Green Man 82, 83
    Columbarium/ dovecote 82
    Holy Well 81
    Knights Templar and 79, 81–84
Gill, Eric 120
Golden Valley 2, 127, 133, 134
Goodrich 146–148, 153, 154
Goodrick-Clarke, Nicholas 124
Gospel Pass 123
Great Malvern 71, 72
Green Man 59, 82, 83, 124, 139, 140
Glyndwr, Owain 2, 158

Hay-on-Wye 107–113, 122–126, 143, 146
    Back Fold 112
    Bluff 114, 115
    Castle 109–113, 160
    Church 115, 123
    Festival 109
Hentland monastery 150
Hereford
    All Saints Church 24, 28, 29
    Blackfriars Monastery 90–92
    Cathedral 12, 21–27, 75, 78, 133
        gatehouse 21
    Church Street 25
    East Street 106
    Plas Gwyn 73
    Victoria Suspension Bridge 23
Herefordshire School of Romanesque Sculpture 138
Hergest Court 54–59
Heron, Mike 11
Hill, Sophie 21
Hinsley, Chris 89
Holy Grail, The 79
hops/ hop-picking 40–44
Hound of the Baskervilles 2, 53, 55–57

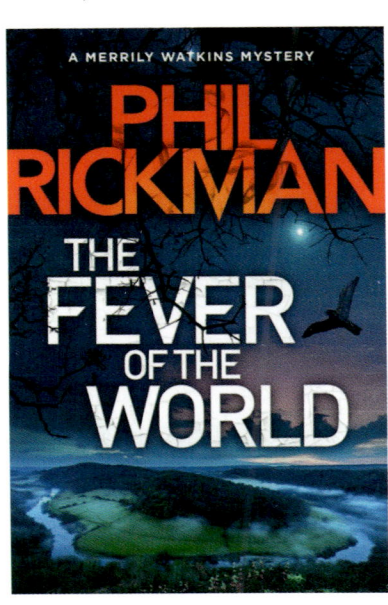

Hutchinson, Thomas 97

Imbolc 31

James, M.R. 77–79, 84, 131
Jenkins, Bob 55
    Thomas 50
Joyce, William 124

Kempley (old) Church 46, 47
Kenchester – *see Magnis*
Kilpeck
    Castle 140, 141
    Church 29, 135–140
King, Stephen 131, 155
Kington 53, 55, 56, 59, 60, 156
    Church 55, 56
Kinnersley Castle 58, 124
    Church 104, 106
Kirkpatrick, John 142
Knight, Prof. Bernard 46
Knight's Frome 40
Knights Hospitaller 81, 82
Knights Templar 77, 79, 81–84

Laudun, Sir William 131–133
Leather, Ella Mary 9, 10, 56, 85, 93, 113, 132, 134
Ledwardine 3, 5, 6, 8, 10, 22, 45, 87, 92
Lee, Patrick Jasper 44
Leland, John 97
Lewis, Jodie 30
Lewis Stempel, John 140
ley lines 23, 24, 25, 29, 73, 148, 149, 152
Little Malvern Priory 71, 72
Llanthony Priory 117–120, 123, 159
Llanwarne Church 36, 37
Lucan, Lord 2, 124
Ludlow 61–67
    Castle 61–63
        Hanging Tower 61–64
    Feather's Hotel 65
    St Laurence's Church 63, 65, 66
        Palmers' Guild 66
    St Leonard's Graveyard 64
Lyon, Nina 139
Lyne, Joseph Leycester 117

MacBride/ McBryde, Gwen 77, 78
    James 78
Madley 150
Magnis (Kenchester) 97, 99, 106
Malvern Hills 1, 39, 40, 70, 71, 72, 74, 75, 123
Mansell Lacy Church 105, 106
Map, Walter 131–134
Meyrick, Sir Samuel Rush 153, 154
Michell, John 25, 75,
Midsummer Hill 69, 71
Moorman, Mary 145, 146
morris dancing 140, 142
Much Marcle 10, 46, 49

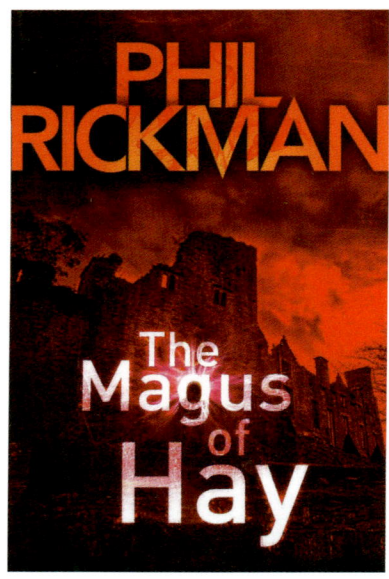

Newman, Cardinal 76
Nown, Graham 140

Old Hindwell 34, 36
Old Radnor Church 33
Oldfield, Mike 156
Owen, Revd Huw 22, 27

Palmer, Samuel 144
Parry, Gomer 2, 3, 14, 59, 126, 140, 155
Peibio, King 150
Pembridge 5–7
Pepper, Bell 61, 64
Phelps, David 133

Pilleth 157, 158
Powell, Edgar 10
Presteigne 58, 156–158
Price, Revd Philip 50

Queen Stone, Huntsham 93, 146–149,
    152–154

Radnor Forest vi, 1, 31–36, 122
Raglan, Lady 139
Robinson, Fletcher 53, 54
    Lol 13, 14, 25, 39, 40, 76, 99, 106, 135,
    142, 161
Romanies 43, 44
Ross-on-Wye 36, 49–52, 144
Rotherwas 88, 89, 92, 93
    Chapel 88
    Ribbon – *see Dinedor Serpent*
Rushdie, Salman 2

Salisbury Plain 145, 146
Sandford, Jeremy 122
SAS 22, 72, 95, 99–101
Seven Sisters, The 152
St Dubricius 149, 150, 152
St George & the Dragon 101, 102
St Michael, churches dedicated to 31,
    33–36, 81
St Thomas Cantilupe 21, 27
Sheelagh-na-gig 29, 124
Smart, Abbot John 158
Smith, Greenough 53, 54
Snodhill Castle 127–132, 134
Spicer, Syd 100
Stanner Hall Hotel 60
    Rocks 60
Stashower, Daniel 54
Stoke Lacy 69, 70
Stoker, Bram 131
Stretford, Church of St Cosmas & Damian 24,
    29, 30, 58
Stukeley, William 97
Sykes, Revd Graham 36, 38
Symonds Yat 49, 97, 144–146, 148–150

Tanworth-in-Arden 13, 14
Taylor, Michael 15

Tintern Abbey 145, 152
Turner, J.M.W. 144
Tomen Castle 32, 33
Traherne, Thomas 11–13
Twelfth Night 10

Underhowle 49

vampires 43, 44, 131–134
Vaughan, family 56, 57, 59
    Ellen 56
    Jenny 59
    Robert Roger, MP 59
    Silvanus, Revd 57
    Thomas ('Black') 54–56, 59
Vortigern 150
Virgin Mary, vision of 119–121

Wadsworth, Canon Michael 17, 19, 20
Walker, Bishop Dominic 18
Wansell, Geoffrey 46
wassailing 10, 11
Watkins, Alfred 2, 23–25, 73, 75, 106, 147–149
    Jane 2, 8, 87, 92, 149
    Merrily 3, 5, 8, 13–15, 17, 21, 22, 45, 61,
    69, 70, 76, 77, 82, 100, 124, 160
Weir Gardens 96, 97
Weobley 5, 7, 10
Wern Derys standing stone 93, 94
West, Fred 45, 46, 49
    Rosemary 45, 46, 49
Weston under Penyard 52
Whiteleafed Oak 75, 76
Wigmore
    Abbey 158
    Castle 159
    Shewstone 157
Williams, John (farmer) 54
    Fr Richard 123
Wordsworth, Dorothy 96, 101, 145, 146
    William 95–97, 101, 144–146
Wychehill 70, 72
Wye, River 22, 23, 89, 96, 97, 111, 113, 115,
    143–146, 148–150

Yazor Church 104, 106

ALSO AVAILABLE FROM LOGASTON PRESS

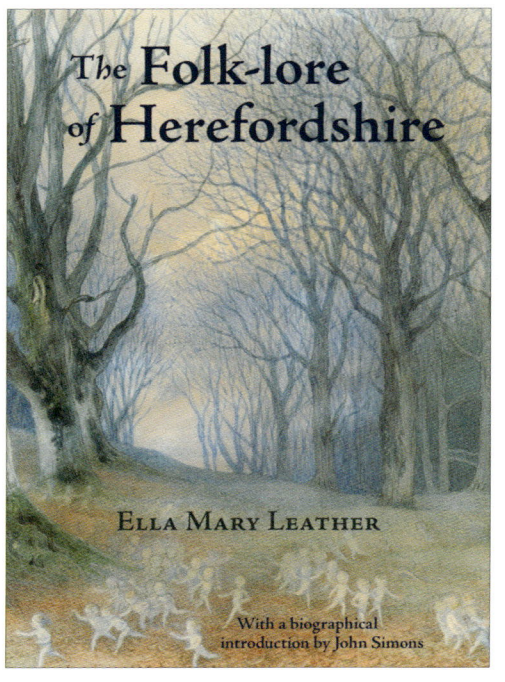

The Folk-lore of Herefordshire
by Ella Mary Leather
with a biographical introduction by John Simons

A new edition of this classic work, first published in 1912, and widely regarded as one of the finest books on English folklore ever written. This edition includes previously unseen photographs by Ella herself, together with an introductory essay by local historian John Simons who lives in the Leathers' old house in Weobley.

Paperback, £15
368 pages, 242 x 171 mm
50 mono illustrations
ISBN: 978-1-910839-29-4

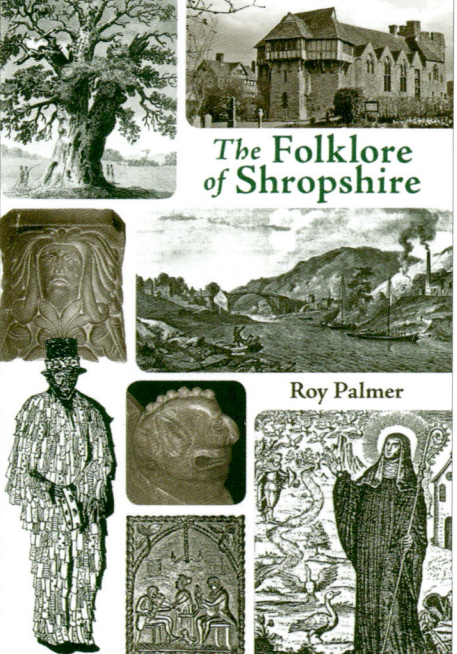

The Folklore of Shropshire
by Roy Palmer

A major folklore of the county by an acknowledged expert in the field (Roy has written folklores of Radnorshire, Herefordshire and Monmouthshire). Presented in eleven themed chapters, *The Folklore of Shropshire* contains a rich store of tales about tunnels and mark stones, giants and dragons, bull and bear baiting, 'cunning folk' and bountiful cows, Edric the Wild, 'burning the mawkin' and wife selling.

Paperback, £15
352 pages, 234 x 156 mm
250 mono illustrations
ISBN: 978-1-904396-16-1